ARTIFICIAL INTELLIGENCE MADE SIMPLE

What you really need to know

Hugo Soto

CONTENTS

Expression

DEDICATION

This book is dedicated to curious minds everywhere, those who are eager to learn and adapt in our rapidly evolving technological landscape. To those who are not intimidated by the complexities of artificial intelligence but instead are inspired by its potential to reshape our world.

It is for the dreamers, the innovators, and the problem-solvers who see AI not as a threat, but as a tool, a partner in building a better future. This dedication is a testament to the power of human ingenuity in harnessing technology for the greater good.

We honor the collaborative spirit and the belief that humanity can wield technological progress ethically and effectively. To everyone who strives to empower themselves through knowledge and understanding: this book is for you.

My hope is that it sparks your curiosity, ignites your imagination, and equips you with the insight and confidence to navigate the AI revolution with purpose. May it serve not just as a guide to the technology itself, but as a compass for its thoughtful and responsible use.

The future is not something to be feared, it is a landscape to be shaped. We invite you to join us in the journey.

INTRODUCTION

Artificial intelligence is no longer a futuristic fantasy; it's woven into the fabric of our daily lives. From the personalized recommendations on your streaming services to the voice assistants on your smartphone, AI is quietly yet powerfully shaping our experiences.

But beyond convenience and entertainment, AI's influence reaches into nearly every sector—transforming healthcare, transportation, finance, education, and even creativity. Understanding AI is no longer a luxury; it's a necessity.

This book is your comprehensive yet accessible guide to navigating this transformative technology. We explore the core concepts of AI, explaining complex ideas in plain English. Our focus is on clarity and practical applications, avoiding heavy technical jargon.

You'll learn how AI is changing the workplace, reshaping job markets, and creating new opportunities. We'll also explore the ethical dimensions of this technology, including issues like algorithmic bias, data privacy, and the spread of misinformation.

In addition to theory, this book provides practical, hands-on guidance for using popular AI tools such as ChatGPT and Midjourney. You'll gain valuable skills to harness these technologies in your personal and professional life.

Through real-world examples, case studies, and expert insights, we aim to paint a well-rounded picture of what AI can do today —and what it may enable tomorrow. But most of all, my goal is to empower you. I want you to not only understand AI, but to feel confident participating in its evolution with purpose and integrity.

So let's begin this journey together, uncovering the mysteries of artificial intelligence and unlocking its transformative potential.

PREFACE

Artificial intelligence. The very term conjures images of sentient robots, dystopian futures, and the looming specter of technological singularity—ideas often fueled more by science fiction than scientific fact. But the reality of AI is far more nuanced and, frankly, far more accessible than many people believe.

This book cuts through the hype and the fear-mongering to offer a clear, straightforward explanation of what AI is, how it works, and—most importantly—how it impacts your life today and will continue to shape your future.

We've designed this guide with the non-expert in mind. No background in computer science or mathematics is required. Using conversational language, real-world examples, and relatable analogies, we aim to demystify even the most complex concepts.

Whether you're a concerned citizen, a curious student, a forward-thinking professional, or simply someone who wants to understand the technology transforming our world, this book is your essential guide. Our goal is to empower you with practical insights, actionable strategies, and a future-readiness checklist to help you thrive in an AI-driven world.

By the time you finish reading, we hope you'll not only understand AI more clearly, but also feel confident in your ability to harness its potential—both personally and professionally. This isn't about passively witnessing the AI revolution; it's about taking an active role in shaping its future.

Let's begin.

ARTIFICIAL INTELLIGENCE MADE SIMPLE

DEFINING AI: SEPARATING FACT FROM FICTION

Artificial intelligence. The term brings to mind sentient robots, self-aware computers, and a future where machines surpass human intelligence. Science fiction has shaped a powerful blend of fascination and fear, often distorting our understanding of AI. But the reality of AI today is far more nuanced—and in many ways, less dramatic—than popular culture would have us believe.

This chapter aims to separate science from science fiction. We'll offer a clear and accessible definition of AI while debunking common myths along the way.

One of the most important distinctions is between hype and reality. Media narratives often portray AI as a single, all-powerful force poised to transform the world overnight. That's misleading. AI isn't a single technology. It's a broad and evolving field composed of many techniques, tools, and applications. Imagine a toolbox: some tools are specialized and extremely effective in narrow contexts, while others are more general but still nowhere near human-level intelligence.

Let's start with the most common form of AI today: narrow AI, also called weak AI. These systems are designed to perform a specific task very well. For instance, your email's spam filter is a type of narrow AI. So are the recommendation engines on Netflix or Spotify, or the facial recognition software used to unlock your smartphone. These systems are highly capable at their designated tasks, but they can't operate outside their programming or adapt to new situations on their own.

In contrast, general AI—or strong AI—refers to the hypothetical development of machines with human-level cognitive abilities. A general AI would be capable of learning, reasoning, problem-solving, and adapting across a wide range of tasks, just like a human. As of now, general AI does not exist. Despite progress in several areas of AI research, we are still far from building machines that can match human intelligence in a comprehensive, flexible way. Films like *Her* or *Ex Machina* portray this kind of AI—systems that exhibit emotional intelligence, nuanced understanding, and even consciousness. These depictions remain firmly in the realm of fiction.

Then there's the concept of superintelligence—AI that would surpass human intelligence in every domain, including creativity, decision-making, and emotional awareness. This idea is the subject of both excitement and concern among researchers and philosophers. While some experts warn of the risks of unchecked superintelligence, others highlight its potential benefits. Importantly, superintelligence is not something we're on the verge of achieving. It remains a theoretical possibility, not a present reality. Discussions about it often veer into philosophical territory, touching on safety, ethics, and what it really means to be intelligent.

To fully appreciate where AI stands today, it's helpful to briefly explore its history. The roots of AI stretch back to the mid-20th century, when pioneers like Alan Turing began laying the theoretical groundwork. The early decades were filled with bold optimism, especially as computers began solving mathematical problems and playing games like chess. But the field also experienced repeated setbacks. These "AI winters" were periods when progress stalled, funding declined, and public enthusiasm waned, largely due to the limits of computing power and the immaturity of early algorithms.

The tide began to turn in the late 20th and early 21st centuries. Several key developments—faster processors, vast data availability, and more sophisticated algorithms—helped spark a new era of AI innovation. At the heart of this resurgence is machine learning, a method that allows computers to learn from data rather than relying on hardcoded instructions. These systems identify patterns, adapt to new inputs, and improve over time, leading to major breakthroughs in areas like image recognition, language translation, and speech processing.

Today's AI renaissance owes much to the accessibility and impact of machine learning. The ability to train powerful models on enormous datasets has transformed industries from healthcare and finance to education and entertainment. Often, these technologies operate quietly in the background, subtly influencing our decisions and experiences. Understanding how they work—and where they fall short—is essential in today's world.

So what exactly is AI? At its core, artificial intelligence refers to computer systems capable of performing tasks that typically require human intelligence. This includes everything from recognizing speech and images to making recommendations, forecasting outcomes, or playing strategy games. However, it's important not to anthropomorphize AI. Machines do not feel, think, or understand in the way humans do. They simulate intelligence through pattern recognition and data processing, not through consciousness or emotion. Recognizing this difference helps keep our expectations grounded.

As AI continues to evolve, its definitions and boundaries may shift. New techniques will emerge. Capabilities will expand.

But fundamentally, AI remains a set of tools—a powerful and growing collection of technologies designed to solve problems and automate tasks with increasing efficiency.

Separating fact from fiction is the first step toward using these tools wisely. Only by understanding both the potential and the limitations of today's AI can we make informed, responsible decisions about how to shape its future. The story of AI is still being written, and we all have a role to play in what comes next.

AI'S BUILDING BLOCKS: ALGORITHMS, DATA, AND MACHINE LEARNING

Let's delve into the core components that make AI systems work. At the most fundamental level, artificial intelligence is built upon three key pillars: algorithms, data, and machine learning. Think of it like baking a cake—the recipe is the algorithm, the ingredients are the data, and the act of baking and adjusting the recipe based on the result is machine learning.

Algorithms are sets of instructions that tell a computer what to do. They are precise, step-by-step procedures, much like a recipe in a cookbook. A simple algorithm might sort a list of numbers by comparing each item and arranging them in ascending order. More complex algorithms drive advanced AI systems, but the core principle remains the same: a structured series of operations designed to achieve a particular outcome. These algorithms are not created at random—they are carefully crafted by engineers and scientists using knowledge from mathematics, statistics, and computer science.

The effectiveness of any algorithm depends on its clarity, efficiency, and appropriateness for the task at hand. A poorly designed algorithm might give inaccurate results or take so long to compute that it becomes unusable in real-world settings.

Equally important is the quality of the data—the "ingredients" of AI. AI systems learn from data, and their performance improves as they are exposed to larger and higher-quality datasets. Data can take many forms: images, text, numbers, audio recordings, or sensor readings—anything that can be represented digitally. For example, a facial recognition system learns to identify faces by analyzing millions of images tagged with individual identities. These tagged images serve as training data, allowing the algorithm to detect patterns in facial features. If the dataset contains blurry images or poor labeling, the system's accuracy drops. Worse, if the dataset reflects existing social biases, the algorithm can learn and even amplify those biases. This is a serious concern and a central focus of current AI research.

So how does an AI system actually learn from this data? This is where machine learning enters the picture. Machine learning isn't about programming rules by hand—it's about enabling systems to identify patterns and infer rules from data on their own.

Imagine teaching a child to recognize a cat. You wouldn't define "cat" using a detailed set of rules; instead, you'd show them many pictures of cats and highlight their common features— fur, whiskers, pointy ears. Over time, the child learns through exposure and observation. Machine learning works in a similar way. Algorithms process the data, recognize patterns, and build models that can make predictions or decisions based on new information.

There are several types of machine learning, each suited to different tasks:

- **Supervised learning** involves training the model on labeled data—datasets where each input is paired with the correct answer. This is like showing the child pictures of animals labeled as "cat" or "not cat."

- **Unsupervised learning** works with unlabeled data, allowing the system to detect patterns or groupings on its own. This is similar to letting the child explore images without guidance and finding commonalities.

- **Reinforcement learning** involves learning through trial and error, with feedback in the form of rewards or penalties. Imagine a child receiving praise when they identify a cat correctly and a gentle correction when they mistake a dog for a cat.

The choice of learning type and algorithm depends on the task and the nature of the data. A spam filter, for instance, typically uses supervised learning on labeled emails. A recommendation engine might use unsupervised learning to group users with similar preferences. Game-playing AIs like those used in chess or Go often rely on reinforcement learning, refining their strategies by playing thousands of games and adjusting based on outcomes.

Take facial recognition again as an example. These systems use advanced algorithms to analyze pixel patterns, measuring the distance between facial landmarks like the eyes and nose. Many such systems rely on **deep learning**, a type of machine learning that uses artificial neural networks to identify complex patterns in vast amounts of data. Deep learning has enabled dramatic improvements in face identification, though it also inherits the same risks of bias if the training data is not diverse and representative.

Another powerful application of AI is **natural language processing (NLP)**, which allows computers to understand

and generate human language. Tools like chatbots, virtual assistants, and real-time translators rely on algorithms that interpret grammar, meaning, and context. These systems are trained on huge datasets of text, helping them learn everything from formal writing to slang and idiomatic expressions. The rise of large language models like GPT-3 and GPT-4 has demonstrated just how far NLP has come. However, concerns about misinformation, bias, and the ethical use of these tools remain prominent and unresolved.

While the mechanics behind AI can be complex, the foundational concepts are straightforward. Algorithms provide the instructions. Data provides the raw material. Machine learning transforms both into intelligent behavior. The true power of AI lies not in any one component, but in the interaction between them. When combined effectively, they enable systems to perform tasks once thought to require human intelligence.

But it's essential to remember that AI is not magic. These systems are tools. They reflect the data they're trained on, the decisions made by their designers, and the assumptions baked into their algorithms. Understanding these building blocks is key to using AI responsibly. As technology continues to evolve, so too must our awareness of its ethical, societal, and economic impacts.

Ultimately, the future of AI depends not only on innovation, but on careful consideration of its consequences. By understanding how AI works—and how it can go wrong—we place ourselves in a better position to shape a future in which this technology benefits everyone.

TYPES OF AI: NARROW, GENERAL, AND SUPERINTELLIGENCE

Now that we've covered the fundamental building blocks of AI—algorithms, data, and machine learning—let's turn our attention to the different types of AI systems. One of the most useful ways to classify AI is by its scope and capability. Broadly speaking, AI can be divided into three types: narrow (or weak) AI, general (or strong) AI, and superintelligence.

Narrow AI is the most common type in use today. Also called weak AI, these systems are designed to perform a single task —or a narrow range of tasks—very effectively. You've likely interacted with narrow AI through digital assistants like Siri, Alexa, or Google Assistant. These tools can understand voice commands, deliver information, and carry out specific functions such as setting reminders or playing music. However, they operate strictly within the boundaries of their programming. They can't compose a novel, solve unrelated mathematical problems, or engage in deep, spontaneous conversations outside of their predefined parameters.

Other examples include spam filters, recommendation systems

on platforms like Netflix or Amazon, and image recognition tools used in self-driving cars. These systems excel at what they're built to do, but they lack the flexibility and broad reasoning abilities of a human being. Their intelligence is narrowly focused and specialized.

The limitations of narrow AI are easy to spot. A chess-playing AI might outperform a grandmaster but wouldn't be able to fold laundry or understand a joke. These systems are designed around curated datasets and tailored algorithms, which optimize performance within strict confines. If asked to operate outside those parameters, they often fail. While narrow AI is powerful and highly useful, it highlights the gap between today's technologies and the kind of adaptive, general-purpose intelligence we associate with human beings.

General AI, also referred to as strong AI or artificial general intelligence (AGI), represents a significant leap forward. AGI would be capable of human-level cognition—it could learn, reason, solve problems, adapt to new situations, and even demonstrate creativity and emotional awareness. A system like this could function effectively across multiple domains, much like a person.

However, AGI remains a theoretical concept. We have not yet created a system that can match human intelligence in a general, flexible way. The barriers are substantial. We still don't fully understand how the human brain works, which makes it incredibly difficult to replicate. Moreover, developing algorithms that can generalize knowledge across diverse contexts and apply it dynamically is an unsolved problem. AGI would also require computing architectures far more advanced than those available today.

Beyond the technical challenges, AGI raises serious ethical and societal questions. How would we ensure that such a system acts in alignment with human values? What safeguards would be necessary to prevent misuse or unintended consequences? These are not just engineering problems; they are deeply philosophical questions that demand input from ethicists, policymakers, and society at large.

Despite the uncertainties, the promise of AGI is compelling. It could revolutionize fields like science, medicine, and environmental management. But the risks are equally profound, particularly if such systems were to act autonomously in unpredictable ways. Responsible development, clear oversight, and global cooperation will be essential to guide this path.

Superintelligence lies beyond AGI and refers to an AI that surpasses human intelligence in every measurable way. Such a system would be capable of making decisions, solving problems, and generating ideas at levels far beyond human comprehension. It could drive enormous advancements in knowledge, innovation, and problem-solving.

At the same time, superintelligence presents some of the most serious and speculative risks. If such a system were to operate beyond our control or misinterpret human intentions, it could have unintended or even catastrophic consequences. This concern is a recurring theme in both academic debate and popular culture. While some believe superintelligence could be the key to solving humanity's greatest challenges, others warn of existential threats if its development is not carefully managed.

The conversation around superintelligence is filled with hypothetical scenarios, many of them based on unknowns. That's why it's important to approach this topic with both curiosity and caution. We should neither dismiss its potential nor assume we fully understand the implications. The development of highly advanced AI demands thoughtful planning, transparent dialogue, and proactive ethical frameworks.

It's also worth noting that the boundaries between narrow AI, general AI, and superintelligence are not always cleanly defined. The progression from one level to the next may not be linear. In fact, increasingly powerful narrow AI systems could, over time, lay the groundwork for AGI. Similarly, breakthroughs in AGI could eventually lead to superintelligent systems. The path forward will be shaped not only by technological breakthroughs, but by the choices we make as a society.

Ongoing research is vital for understanding the opportunities and risks of each type of AI. Only by considering the broader ethical, social, and economic impacts can we ensure that AI evolves in a direction that serves humanity's best interests.

The journey toward more advanced AI systems requires ongoing reassessment of our goals, responsibilities, and values. As we push the boundaries of what machines can do, we must also deepen our commitment to ensuring these technologies support human well-being. Open collaboration among researchers, governments, and the public will be essential. The future of AI is not inevitable—it is something we shape together.

AI IN EVERYDAY LIFE: UNVEILING THE INVISIBLE INTELLIGENCE

We've explored the foundational concepts of artificial intelligence and the major classifications—narrow AI, general AI, and the speculative frontier of superintelligence. Now let's shift our attention to something more tangible: how AI integrates into our daily routines. Often invisible yet deeply embedded in our experiences, AI shapes how we live, work, and interact with the world. It's no longer a futuristic fantasy; it's the silent force running beneath many of the conveniences we take for granted.

Think about your morning. Did you wake to the gentle chime of a smart alarm clock? These devices analyze your sleep patterns to wake you at the optimal time for alertness. Did you scroll through a newsfeed curated just for you? That feed is powered by algorithms predicting your interests based on your past behavior. Perhaps your smart coffee maker prepared your morning brew, heating the water to your preferred temperature before you even stepped into the kitchen.

Each of these seemingly simple actions is powered by

sophisticated AI systems. While they may feel trivial, they illustrate just how deeply AI is embedded in even the most mundane aspects of modern life. Understanding how these technologies work allows us to engage with them more thoughtfully and responsibly.

Take, for example, your Netflix recommendations. The algorithm doesn't just suggest random shows. It uses machine learning models that analyze your viewing history, ratings, and patterns among users with similar preferences. Over time, it constructs a complex user profile to predict what you'll enjoy next. This tailored experience enhances satisfaction and keeps you engaged, yet it operates almost entirely in the background.

Music streaming platforms like Spotify and Apple Music do something similar. Their recommendation engines study your listening history, favorite genres, and even the time of day you tend to play certain types of music. The result is a personalized experience that evolves with your preferences. You don't need to understand how the system works to benefit from it— but knowing the mechanics helps us become more mindful consumers.

GPS navigation is another example of AI in action. What seems like a straightforward task—getting from Point A to Point B— involves a web of algorithms analyzing traffic, road closures, construction zones, and real-time delays. As conditions change, the system updates your route on the fly, optimizing your travel time. This kind of adaptability is a hallmark of AI's strength: real-time, data-driven decision-making in dynamic environments.

In the home, AI is transforming how we live. Smart speakers like Alexa and Google Home respond to voice commands, allowing you to control lighting, temperature, music, and even appliances. Smart refrigerators can track inventory, suggest recipes, and reorder groceries when supplies run low. These interconnected devices form the foundation of the "smart home," offering increased convenience and efficiency. They automate routine tasks and free up mental bandwidth for more meaningful activities.

AI's influence goes beyond consumer electronics. In healthcare, algorithms assist in diagnostics by analyzing medical images like X-rays and MRIs, helping doctors detect issues earlier and with greater accuracy. AI accelerates drug discovery, predicts patient outcomes, and helps personalize treatment plans. These applications are transforming healthcare delivery—but they also raise serious questions about data privacy, transparency, and the need for rigorous validation.

While the convenience of AI is compelling, it's important to recognize its potential downsides. Personalized recommendations can create *filter bubbles*, limiting our exposure to diverse viewpoints and reinforcing biases. The data collected by smart devices raises legitimate privacy concerns, from how information is stored to who has access to it. And as AI systems take on critical responsibilities—like autonomous driving or medical decision-making—the stakes grow higher. We must ensure these systems are reliable, secure, and tested under real-world conditions.

One emerging concern is the rise of *deepfakes*—realistic but fake videos generated by AI. These videos can imitate people with startling accuracy, making it difficult to distinguish fact from fiction. Deepfakes have been used to spread misinformation, damage reputations, and even incite unrest. Addressing this challenge requires a combination of technological solutions, public awareness, and legal frameworks.

As AI continues to shape our lives, understanding both its benefits and limitations becomes essential. We need to recognize how it influences our choices, question the assumptions behind the systems we use, and engage in informed discussions about the ethical implications. This requires ongoing education, critical thinking, and transparency from those developing the technology.

Looking ahead, AI is poised to become even more deeply integrated into society. That brings opportunities—to improve productivity, enhance healthcare, and personalize education —but it also presents challenges. We must ensure that AI systems are developed responsibly, with safeguards that align with human values. Achieving that vision will require not just innovation, but collaboration across disciplines, industries, and borders.

This journey will demand thoughtful stewardship, clear ethical principles, and a commitment to putting people first. With careful guidance, AI can become a force that empowers rather than dominates, supports rather than controls. The future of AI is not just about what we build—it's about how, and why, we build it.

THE FUTURE OF AI: PREDICTIONS AND POSSIBILITIES

As we've seen, AI is already deeply integrated into our daily lives. But what lies ahead? While predicting the future is never an exact science, current trends and emerging technologies give us meaningful insight into where AI is headed. Rather than indulging in science fiction or fear-based speculation, this chapter explores realistic and plausible trajectories based on today's developments and tomorrow's needs.

One of the most promising fields for AI innovation is **healthcare**. We've already touched on AI's role in diagnostics and drug discovery, but its potential reaches much further. Imagine AI-powered personal health assistants that monitor vital signs in real time, provide early warnings for potential health issues, and recommend lifestyle changes to prevent disease. With access to an individual's genetic profile and medical history, AI could tailor treatment plans for maximum effectiveness and minimal side effects.

AI could also enhance surgical precision, making procedures less invasive and recovery times shorter. Assistive devices and intelligent prosthetics might offer life-changing mobility and independence to people with disabilities. However, these breakthroughs come with challenges. Protecting sensitive health data is critical, and systems must be rigorously tested to prevent bias in diagnoses and treatments. Ethical concerns also emerge when AI is involved in life-or-death decisions. This demands transparent regulation and interdisciplinary collaboration between scientists, doctors, ethicists, and policymakers.

Transportation is another domain on the brink of transformation. Self-driving cars, already in development and testing, promise safer roads, fewer traffic jams, and more efficient fuel usage. AI-driven traffic management could reduce commute times by dynamically rerouting vehicles in real time. Autonomous delivery services may revolutionize logistics, enhancing supply chain speed and reliability.

Yet widespread adoption will depend on establishing robust safety standards, preventing cybersecurity threats, and making thoughtful decisions about liability and human oversight. Job displacement in industries like trucking and ride-sharing must also be addressed, calling for retraining initiatives and economic support for affected workers.

In the realm of **communication**, AI continues to evolve. Translation tools are breaking down language barriers, and virtual assistants are becoming more responsive and intelligent. These tools promise a more personalized, seamless communication experience—tailoring messages, responses, and content based on context and user behavior.

But this growing personalization brings new risks. The rise of *deepfakes*—AI-generated videos and audio that convincingly imitate real people—poses a serious threat to trust and authenticity. These tools can be used to spread misinformation, manipulate public opinion, or damage reputations. Combating this misuse will require a mix of technological countermeasures, strong media literacy, and clear legal and ethical frameworks.

More broadly, **AI will reshape nearly every sector of society**, from education and finance to agriculture and manufacturing. Automation will replace some jobs while creating new ones, especially in areas that require oversight, design, and ethical governance of AI systems. This shift demands significant investment in education, workforce retraining, and digital literacy to ensure inclusive participation in an AI-driven economy.

As AI becomes more powerful, the **ethical stakes rise**. Who is responsible when an AI makes a harmful decision? How do we prevent discrimination embedded in algorithms? How do we build systems that reflect diverse values rather than just the priorities of their developers?

Preparing for the future means going beyond technical innovation. We need policy, regulation, and civic engagement to ensure AI development remains aligned with democratic principles. Education systems must evolve to teach not only technical skills, but also critical thinking and digital ethics. Transparent development processes and public accountability will be essential to prevent abuse and build trust.

The future is not something that simply happens to us—it's something we help create. Our collective choices will determine whether AI serves as a tool for empowerment or a source of division. That means we must approach it with both ambition and caution, embracing its benefits while addressing its risks.

This journey requires more than smart engineering—it demands **shared responsibility**. Developers must build with fairness and transparency. Policymakers must implement frameworks that protect individuals and encourage innovation. Citizens must stay informed and engaged, asking hard questions and pushing for ethical practices.

Global cooperation is also essential. AI is a global force, and its development must reflect a commitment to shared values. International research collaborations, open-access models, and joint standards can help ensure that the benefits of AI are widely distributed rather than concentrated in the hands of a few.

The future of AI is not a fixed destination—it is a constantly evolving story. Every decision we make, every system we build, and every policy we implement adds a new chapter. The real question isn't whether AI will change the world—it's how we will guide that change.

We stand at a crossroads. With careful foresight, ethical stewardship, and a commitment to humanity's well-being, AI can be one of the most powerful tools of progress ever created. The future of AI is not just about machines—it's about people, values, and the kind of world we want to build together.

AI'S IMPACT ON JOBS: AUTOMATION AND NEW OPPORTUNITIES

The rapid advancement of artificial intelligence is reshaping not only our everyday experiences but also the fundamental nature of work. Its impact is multifaceted—disrupting certain job sectors while simultaneously creating new ones. This shift, though potentially unsettling, also presents an opportunity for societal growth, provided it is met with strategic planning and proactive adaptation.

One of the most visible effects of AI on employment is automation. Repetitive, manual tasks that once formed the core of many industries are increasingly being handled by AI-powered systems. In manufacturing, robotic arms guided by advanced algorithms now execute tasks with speed, precision, and tireless consistency. Assembly lines that once required large numbers of human workers are becoming more efficient and less reliant on manual labor. Similar automation trends are evident in warehousing and logistics, where automated guided vehicles (AGVs) and robotic sorting systems improve accuracy and speed.

However, automation doesn't only mean job replacement—it also means job enhancement. AI systems can relieve workers of routine tasks, allowing humans to focus on creative, strategic, or supervisory roles. For example, factory workers may shift from physical assembly to managing automated systems, identifying issues, and driving process improvements. While this transition requires reskilling, it also holds the promise of greater productivity and job satisfaction.

The **customer service** industry is undergoing a comparable transformation. AI-powered chatbots and virtual assistants now manage routine inquiries, allowing human agents to focus on more complex, empathetic interactions. Though some traditional roles may be phased out, new opportunities are emerging for professionals who design and optimize these systems, analyze customer data, and improve user experience.

In **healthcare**, the influence of AI is growing steadily. AI tools assist doctors in diagnosing diseases earlier and more accurately, leading to better patient outcomes. But rather than replacing doctors, these tools augment human expertise. Physicians remain central to healthcare delivery, especially when interpreting AI-generated insights or managing complex cases. The growing demand for professionals who can integrate AI into clinical workflows underscores the need for training in both medicine and technology.

The **finance sector** is also seeing sweeping changes. Algorithmic trading platforms make rapid investment decisions based on market data, while AI systems detect fraud by identifying subtle transaction anomalies. While some traditional roles may become obsolete, new roles in data science, AI ethics, and risk management are expanding rapidly. These emerging positions are essential to ensure the safe, transparent, and ethical use of AI in financial operations.

More broadly, AI is not only displacing jobs—it's creating entirely new professions. Careers in AI development, machine learning engineering, data analysis, and AI ethics are growing rapidly. As companies deploy more AI tools, the demand for talent with expertise in programming, modeling, and ethical decision-making continues to rise. These roles require both technical proficiency and a deep understanding of how AI affects people and systems.

To meet this demand, **education and training** must evolve. Schools and universities need to incorporate AI-focused curricula that build digital literacy, computational thinking, and interdisciplinary knowledge. Just as important are reskilling and upskilling programs for workers whose roles are at risk of automation. These initiatives should be accessible, affordable, and aligned with market needs to ensure inclusive participation in the evolving workforce.

Governments play a critical role in shaping this transition. Public investment in digital infrastructure and workforce development is essential. Policymakers must also design regulatory frameworks that protect workers, promote fair labor practices, and guard against bias in AI systems. Supporting research in AI ethics and responsible deployment will be key to ensuring that technological advancement aligns with democratic values.

Businesses, too, must step up. Companies can ease the impact of automation by investing in employee training, fostering a culture of continuous learning, and offering internal mobility. Forward-thinking employers understand that supporting their workforce through this transition strengthens loyalty, resilience, and long-term success.

The future of work in the age of AI is not about resisting change—it's about **strategically adapting** to it. Embracing lifelong learning, acquiring new skills, and remaining agile are essential traits for success in a dynamic job market. Governments, industries, and educational institutions must collaborate to build systems that support human potential alongside technological progress.

This transition won't be without challenges, but it offers a chance to create a more flexible, inclusive, and future-ready economy. With careful planning, transparent policies, and a commitment to equitable opportunity, AI can become a catalyst for human advancement rather than a threat to employment.

The question isn't whether AI will affect jobs—it's how we choose to respond. By embracing innovation and putting people at the center of change, we can ensure that technology and humanity grow together, each enhancing the other in a shared vision of progress.

SKILLS FOR THE AI ERA: ADAPTING AND THRIVING IN A CHANGING WORLD

In previous sections, we explored how artificial intelligence is reshaping the workplace—eliminating some roles while creating entirely new opportunities. The key question now is: what skills will help individuals not just survive, but thrive in this evolving environment?

The answer goes beyond a list of technical proficiencies. Success in the AI era demands a blend of **hard and soft skills**, combining specialized knowledge with the adaptability and emotional intelligence needed to navigate uncertainty. This chapter explores the key abilities that will define future-ready professionals in an AI-powered world.

Critical thinking stands at the top of the list. AI systems, no matter how sophisticated, are tools—dependent on humans for design, interpretation, and oversight. The ability to assess information, question assumptions, detect bias, and evaluate sources is vital in a world flooded with data. Whether you're a marketer analyzing AI-generated customer insights or a journalist reviewing AI-curated content, the capacity to think critically is essential to prevent misinformation, flawed strategies, or unintended harm.

Equally vital is **problem-solving**. While AI excels at repetitive tasks and data processing, it struggles with ambiguity, nuance, and unexpected challenges. Human ingenuity remains essential for diagnosing complex issues, crafting creative solutions, and adapting when things go off-script. For instance, a software engineer troubleshooting an AI application must not only understand code but also grasp the broader system context and creatively resolve errors the AI can't anticipate.

Perhaps the most essential attribute is **adaptability**. In a fast-moving technological landscape, the tools we use today may be obsolete tomorrow. The ability to quickly learn new systems, adapt to changing job demands, and embrace continuous learning is a non-negotiable skill. This might mean enrolling in online courses, attending industry workshops, or even pursuing advanced degrees. More important than any single skill is the willingness to learn, unlearn, and relearn—again and again.

Which skills are the least likely to be automated? The answer lies in **deeply human abilities**. Jobs that require **complex interpersonal interaction**, **emotional intelligence**, and **strategic thinking** remain relatively insulated from automation. This includes roles in healthcare, education, counseling, and the arts. While AI may assist doctors in diagnosis or teachers in curriculum design, it cannot replicate empathy, nuanced human communication, or creative vision. These attributes remain distinctly human and therefore essential in a future workplace.

At the same time, **transferable soft skills** like communication, teamwork, leadership, negotiation, and project management continue to hold tremendous value. For example, a data scientist might master complex models, but without the ability to explain results to a non-technical audience, their impact is limited. These interpersonal skills are difficult to automate and remain critical for collaboration in AI-augmented work environments.

On the technical side, **emerging fields focused on AI itself** offer high-growth opportunities. Roles in **data science**, **machine learning, AI ethics, cybersecurity**, and **AI governance** are in high demand. These careers require deep technical understanding and often advanced degrees, but for those without a strong technical background, adjacent roles in policy, compliance, design, and communication are also emerging—particularly around the ethical use of AI.

One key mindset that underpins all of these skills is the **growth mindset**—the belief that abilities can be developed through effort, learning, and persistence. Embracing challenges as opportunities, learning from setbacks, and remaining curious are traits that foster resilience in a rapidly changing world. This mindset is more than motivation; it's a survival skill in a landscape where transformation is constant.

There are also practical steps anyone can take today to future-proof their careers:

- Enroll in online learning platforms like **Coursera**, **edX**, or **Udacity** to gain AI-related skills at any level.

- Attend **workshops and conferences** to learn from experts and network with professionals in emerging fields.

- Start **personal projects** that explore AI tools and technologies, building a tangible portfolio of skills.

- Seek **mentorship** from experienced professionals in your area of interest.

- Join **online communities** and professional networks (such as LinkedIn groups or Discord servers) to stay informed and connected.

The rise of AI should not be a source of fear, but a call to action. By cultivating a versatile skill set that complements

AI capabilities, we position ourselves not just to survive disruption—but to lead through it. The future of work isn't about replacing humans with machines; it's about empowering humans through machines.

With the right mix of skills, an adaptable mindset, and a commitment to lifelong learning, we can step confidently into this new era—ready to shape it rather than be shaped by it.

AI AS A COLLABORATIVE TOOL: HUMAN–AI PARTNERSHIPS

In the previous section, we explored the essential skills required to thrive in an AI-driven workplace. But beyond personal development, one of the most transformative shifts underway is the evolution of work itself—from human effort alone to human–AI collaboration. Rather than seeing AI as a threat or a replacement, the more accurate and productive perspective is to view AI as a **collaborative partner**—a tool that augments our capabilities, enhances productivity, and opens new pathways for creativity and innovation.

This is not a story of humans *versus* machines. It's a story of humans *with* machines.

Consider the field of **medicine**, where AI is already changing how diagnoses are made and treatments are planned. AI systems can analyze medical images with incredible precision, identifying subtle anomalies that may be difficult for the human eye to detect. But this does not replace the physician. The doctor retains the essential role of interpreting results, incorporating a patient's history and context, and making critical decisions.

The AI assists by handling data-intensive analysis, enabling the doctor to focus more on empathy, communication, and holistic care. The result is a collaborative workflow that enhances both efficiency and patient outcomes.

A similar model is playing out in **manufacturing**. Robots now handle repetitive or physically taxing tasks on production lines, reducing workplace injuries and increasing efficiency. Human workers, meanwhile, are shifting into supervisory roles —monitoring systems, maintaining equipment, and innovating new processes. These roles are safer, more engaging, and intellectually fulfilling. The factory of the future doesn't eliminate humans; it transforms their roles into something more strategic and sustainable.

Creative industries offer another compelling example. Tools like Midjourney and DALL·E 2 can generate striking visuals based on text prompts. Yet the artist is still central to the creative process. It is the human who shapes the vision, curates the AI's output, and infuses the final product with emotional depth and nuance. AI becomes a tool for exploration and experimentation, accelerating the design process—but it does not replace imagination or the artist's unique voice.

Even fields traditionally considered deeply human, such as **writing and legal research**, are benefiting from AI assistance. Writers use tools like AI-generated outlines or text suggestions to spark ideas and overcome creative blocks. Lawyers rely on AI to rapidly scan and analyze thousands of legal documents to find relevant precedents. In both cases, the AI supports the human expert—but the critical thinking, ethical judgment, and final decisions remain firmly in human hands.

The success of human–AI partnerships depends on one essential truth: **AI is a tool, not a mind.** It excels at analyzing patterns, processing large volumes of data, and executing predefined tasks. But it lacks the context, intuition, empathy, and moral reasoning that define human intelligence. The real power lies in combining these strengths—using AI to handle what it does best so humans can focus on what only we can do.

To make this collaboration effective, we need to develop not only technical skills, but a new **mindset**. This means:

- Understanding the strengths and limitations of AI tools
- Learning how to prompt, guide, and interpret AI outputs
- Developing communication and collaboration skills for mixed human-AI teams
- Cultivating flexibility and a willingness to learn continuously as technologies evolve

In the future workplace, roles focused solely on repetitive, data-heavy tasks will change dramatically. But positions that require **creativity, critical thinking, emotional intelligence, and problem-solving** will continue to thrive—and become even more essential. Humans will guide, contextualize, and make value-driven decisions based on AI-generated insights.

Of course, these changes also introduce new responsibilities. Organizations must address **ethical concerns** such as fairness, bias, and accountability in AI systems. They must invest in **reskilling and upskilling** workers to help them adapt. And they must foster cultures of **lifelong learning**—providing access to education, mentorship, and professional growth to keep employees competitive and fulfilled.

The future of work is not a zero-sum equation between people and machines. It's a shared venture. A true **partnership**. With human creativity and emotional intelligence guiding the power of AI, we can unlock new levels of productivity, imagination, and impact.

But realizing that vision requires action. It demands that we approach AI with curiosity, not fear. That we commit to ongoing learning. That we build systems and cultures designed not just for efficiency, but for **human flourishing**.

The most valuable skill in this new era won't be programming or technical mastery alone. It will be the ability to collaborate —skillfully, ethically, and creatively—with intelligent machines. When we do that, we won't just adapt to change, we'll lead it.

THE ETHICS OF AI IN THE WORKPLACE: FAIRNESS, BIAS, AND ACCOUNTABILITY

As artificial intelligence becomes increasingly embedded in the workplace, it brings with it not only the promise of greater efficiency and productivity but also a host of complex ethical challenges. These aren't abstract concerns—they're already reshaping hiring practices, employee monitoring, decision-making, and workplace dynamics. Addressing them requires urgent attention, thoughtful action, and a commitment to transparency, fairness, and human dignity.

One of the most urgent issues is **bias and fairness in AI-driven hiring**. Many organizations now use AI tools to scan resumes and screen candidates, with the goal of removing human bias and streamlining the recruitment process. But AI systems are only as impartial as the data on which they are trained. When historical data reflects systemic bias—such as the underrepresentation of women or minorities in certain industries—AI can inherit and even amplify those biases. The outcome? Qualified candidates may be unfairly excluded, not by conscious discrimination, but by flawed algorithms and skewed data.

For example, imagine an AI tool trained on hiring data from a predominantly male tech company. It might learn to favor resumes containing terms more common in male applicants, inadvertently screening out qualified women or members of underrepresented groups. The problem isn't malicious intent; it's uncritical reliance on biased historical patterns. To counter this, companies must develop more representative training datasets, regularly audit algorithms for discriminatory patterns, and maintain **human oversight** throughout the process. Recruiters should play an active role in evaluating AI-assisted decisions—not just approving them blindly.

Another ethical concern lies in **AI-powered workplace surveillance**. From keystroke tracking to facial recognition and sentiment analysis, AI monitoring systems offer employers unprecedented insight into employee behavior. While such systems can boost productivity and identify issues early, they can also erode privacy, create stress, and damage morale. Constant surveillance can make workers feel dehumanized or distrusted, especially if there's little transparency about how the data is collected or used.

Striking the right balance is essential. Employees should be clearly informed about what is being monitored, how that information is used, and what protections are in place. **Data collection should be proportionate, transparent, and legally compliant**, with clear boundaries to prevent misuse. Monitoring should support—not undermine—well-being, productivity, and trust.

Closely tied to these concerns is the question of **accountability**. When AI makes an error, who bears responsibility? Is it the developer who built the algorithm? The company that deployed it? The manager who followed its recommendation? Consider a situation where an AI hiring tool mistakenly filters out a qualified candidate due to biased training data. Who is responsible for that lost opportunity?

To avoid confusion and injustice, organizations need clear accountability frameworks. That includes assigning responsibility for outcomes, implementing mechanisms to correct errors, and providing recourse for those affected. Human oversight must be embedded in every stage of AI deployment, from design and development to implementation and decision-making.

Ethical considerations also extend to **job displacement and worker transitions**. While AI is creating new roles, it is also automating many others. Companies have a responsibility to prepare for these shifts—not by resisting innovation, but by investing in people. This means offering access to **reskilling and upskilling programs** that prepare workers for emerging roles, both technical and non-technical. It's not just about teaching coding; it's about building resilience, adaptability, and problem-solving skills that will remain relevant in an evolving job market.

Governments and businesses must collaborate with educational institutions and workforce development organizations to ensure that opportunities are accessible and inclusive. Proactive planning can ease transitions and reduce the risk of widespread disruption.

In the face of these challenges, **ethical implementation of AI is not an obstacle—it is a responsibility**. Promoting fairness requires robust data governance, transparent algorithm design, and vigilant oversight. Protecting privacy demands clear communication, legal safeguards, and respectful data practices. Ensuring accountability means establishing clear chains of responsibility and recourse. Supporting displaced workers calls for sustained investment in lifelong learning and inclusive growth strategies.

The ethical use of AI is not a one-time project. It is a **continuous process**—one that demands humility, vigilance, and a willingness to evolve. By centering human values in the design and deployment of AI systems, we can build workplaces where technology supports—not supplants—dignity, fairness, and opportunity.

Ultimately, the future of work powered by AI should not be measured solely in efficiency gains, but in how it upholds the principles of equity, trust, and shared progress. The challenge before us is not simply technical—it is profoundly human.

CASE STUDIES: AI IN ACTION ACROSS INDUSTRIES

Artificial intelligence is no longer a theoretical concept confined to research labs—it is actively transforming industries across the globe. This chapter explores how AI is being applied in real-world contexts, highlighting both the achievements and the challenges that come with implementation. These case studies showcase AI's remarkable versatility, its potential to improve human life, and the ethical considerations that demand our attention.

Healthcare is one of the most impactful arenas for AI innovation. AI-powered diagnostic tools are helping medical professionals make faster and more accurate decisions. In radiology, for example, AI algorithms trained on large datasets can analyze X-rays, CT scans, and MRIs to detect subtle anomalies—such as early-stage tumors or micro-fractures—sometimes more accurately than human specialists alone. These tools enable earlier diagnoses, improve patient outcomes, and ease the workload on medical staff.

However, challenges remain. The effectiveness of AI diagnostic tools depends heavily on the quality and diversity of their training data. If datasets are skewed toward certain populations, the system may underperform with patients from underrepresented groups. This raises serious concerns about fairness and equity in healthcare. Moreover, questions about data privacy, consent, and accountability for diagnostic errors must be addressed through clear policies, ongoing human oversight, and rigorous algorithm testing.

In the **financial sector**, AI plays a critical role in fraud detection and risk assessment. Banks and financial institutions manage millions of transactions daily, making real-time fraud detection a formidable challenge. Machine learning algorithms can identify patterns and flag unusual activity far faster than human analysts. AI is also used to assess creditworthiness, forecast market trends, and personalize financial advice.

But these systems are not without ethical concerns. Bias in AI-driven lending practices could result in discriminatory decisions if the models are trained on flawed or unequal historical data. There's also the risk that sophisticated fraudsters could manipulate AI systems. To prevent misuse, financial institutions must prioritize transparency, explainability, and continual monitoring, ensuring that AI decisions can be audited and understood.

In **manufacturing**, AI is revolutionizing operations through **predictive maintenance**. By analyzing sensor data from equipment, AI systems can forecast when a machine is likely to fail, allowing companies to perform preventative maintenance. This minimizes unplanned downtime and optimizes production schedules—critical in high-speed industries like electronics or automotive manufacturing.

These benefits, however, depend on accurate data integration and a deep understanding of each facility's operations. AI systems must be tailored to the specific machines they monitor, and existing workflows may need to be adjusted. Training staff to interpret the AI's insights is also essential to ensure the technology is used effectively and safely.

The **transportation industry** is also undergoing a profound transformation. AI-driven **autonomous vehicles** are no longer the stuff of science fiction. These vehicles rely on complex algorithms to process real-time data from cameras, sensors, and GPS systems, making decisions on navigation and hazard avoidance. The potential benefits are enormous: fewer accidents, reduced traffic congestion, and greater mobility for the elderly and disabled.

Yet, the road to full autonomy is complex. Ensuring safety in unpredictable environments, assigning responsibility for accidents, and managing the economic impact on professional drivers are all critical challenges. Regulatory frameworks must evolve alongside the technology to address these questions responsibly.

In **customer service**, AI-powered **chatbots** and virtual agents are increasingly handling routine inquiries and tasks. These tools can operate 24/7, resolve common issues, and escalate more complex cases to human agents. When implemented thoughtfully, they reduce costs and improve customer satisfaction.

However, poor design can lead to frustration when chatbots fail to understand nuanced language or provide helpful responses. Effective deployment requires extensive training data, natural language processing capabilities, and a seamless handoff process to human support when needed. Ultimately, striking the right balance between automation and personalized human care is key.

These case studies underscore the profound influence AI has across industries. Yet they also serve as a reminder: **AI is not a universal fix**. Every application comes with distinct challenges —related to data quality, algorithm bias, user experience, and ethical oversight. To succeed, AI implementations must be paired with strong governance, transparent policies, and human-centered design.

Moreover, **the societal implications of AI**—including job displacement and the widening skills gap—demand coordinated action. Governments, industries, and educational institutions must work together to develop upskilling programs and ensure that the workforce is equipped to adapt.

The future of AI is filled with promises, but unlocking its full potential requires responsibility, foresight, and inclusion. By learning from early successes and failures, and by keeping human values at the center of innovation, we can build an AI-powered future that benefits all.

AI AS A CREATIVE PARTNER: COLLABORATION AND INSPIRATION

The integration of artificial intelligence into creative endeavors is no longer a futuristic fantasy, it's a rapidly evolving reality. AI is emerging not as a replacement for human creativity, but as a powerful collaborator that expands the boundaries of artistic expression and fuels the imagination. Rather than viewing AI as a threat, we should embrace it as a catalyst for innovation and a source of inspiration that opens new pathways for creative exploration.

Consider the writer grappling with writer's block, staring at a blank screen. AI-powered writing tools, such as GPT-3 and its successors, offer a digital lifeline. These sophisticated language models can generate text based on a prompt, suggesting alternate phrasing, new plot directions, or even entire story segments. The goal isn't for AI to write the story, but to act as a creative springboard, helping the writer overcome obstacles and refine their work. The human author remains in control— selecting, editing, and shaping the AI's suggestions to fit their voice and vision. In this way, AI becomes a brainstorming partner, capable of exploring numerous directions and enhancing the creative process.

This collaboration is iterative. The writer might begin with a rough outline or a few descriptive lines, and the AI responds with expansions, stylistic variations, or surprising twists. The writer then curates these outputs, integrating what works and discarding what doesn't. The process promotes experimentation and exploration, leading to outcomes that might not have emerged through human effort alone. Rather than replacing the storyteller, AI empowers them, enhancing their ability to create richer, more nuanced narratives.

Visual artists are also harnessing the power of AI in innovative ways. Tools like **Midjourney** and **DALL·E 2** generate striking images from simple textual descriptions. An artist can input a vision—a dreamlike forest, a futuristic skyline, or an abstract portrait—and receive a series of images that reflect those ideas. This process helps artists rapidly prototype concepts, explore different styles, and reimagine traditional aesthetics. The artist curates and refines the AI-generated imagery, often combining it with digital or traditional techniques to achieve their final vision. In this model, AI doesn't replace the creative hand; it becomes a versatile extension of it.

The **music industry** is experiencing a similar transformation. AI tools can now compose melodies, harmonies, and rhythms, offering composers fresh material and unexpected musical directions. A musician wrestling with a section of a composition might turn to AI for alternative chord progressions or melodic ideas. The result is not a machine-made song, but a piece of music shaped by human interpretation and artistic intent. AI can break creative stalemates, suggest new genres to explore, and challenge musicians to step outside their comfort zones while leaving final control in the hands of the artist.

Despite these opportunities, the integration of AI into the

creative process is not without complexity. One concern is the risk of **stylistic homogenization**. If AI models are trained predominantly on popular or historically dominant styles, they may reinforce those patterns rather than foster originality. This makes it vital for creators to use AI tools thoughtfully—guiding them with a unique vision and pushing past imitation into innovation.

Another pressing issue involves **authorship and intellectual property**. When an AI generates an image, song, or passage of text, who owns the result? Is it the artist who provided the prompt, the developers who created the algorithm, or some combination of both? As legal frameworks lag behind technological progress, creators must navigate questions of ownership, attribution, and copyright. Clear guidelines and transparent practices are essential to ensure fair use and to honor both human and technological contributions.

It's also important to acknowledge the **limitations of current AI systems**. While they can mimic form, generate variations, and uncover patterns, AI lacks the emotional depth, lived experience, and contextual awareness that give human art its resonance. Great art reflects the complexity of life, the joys, struggles, and contradictions that define human experience. AI cannot replace this; it can only assist in its expression. Used responsibly, AI becomes a tool for amplification, not substitution.

Even so, the creative results already emerging from human–AI collaboration are extraordinary. Writers are exploring new genres, visual artists are reimagining aesthetics, and musicians are composing innovative hybrids of classical and contemporary sound. As AI technology continues to advance, its role in the creative landscape will only deepen—offering more powerful tools for those who dare to experiment, refine, and evolve.

This moment marks the beginning of a new era—**not**

of machines replacing artists, but of machines working alongside them. By combining computational power with human intuition and originality, we can unlock an unprecedented era of creative expression. The future of art will be defined not by humans versus AI, but by **humans with AI—** a partnership built on curiosity, imagination, and a shared drive to explore the unknown.

The journey has only just begun.

AI-GENERATED ART AND MUSIC: EXPLORING NEW FORMS OF EXPRESSION

The rise of AI-generated art and music marks a profound shift in how we understand and experience creativity. No longer confined to human hands or minds, artistic expression now encompasses the computational power of algorithms, giving rise to a unique fusion of human intention and machine execution. This collaboration is spawning new aesthetics, raising compelling ethical questions, and reshaping our perceptions of authorship and originality.

One of the most striking aspects of AI-generated art is its ability to produce visually stunning and often unexpected results. Tools such as **DALL·E 2**, **Midjourney**, and **Stable Diffusion** allow users to enter textual prompts—descriptions of the images they wish to create—and receive outputs that range from photorealistic renderings to abstract, surreal compositions. These systems rely on advanced neural networks trained on massive datasets of images and text, learning to associate language with visual features. When a user submits a prompt, the AI interprets it and generates an image based on these learned associations.

The results can be breathtaking. Some images demonstrate a level of detail and stylistic cohesion that rivals or even surpasses what many digital artists can produce unaided. However, the significance of this technology lies not only in its technical capabilities but also in what it means for artistic style and originality.

Because these models are trained on existing works of art, their outputs often echo established styles. This raises the question: is AI-generated art truly original, or is it simply a sophisticated form of imitation? Some argue that originality resides in the user's conceptual framing—the prompts they choose and the intent behind them. Others see novelty in the AI's unexpected combinations, which can result in surprising visual juxtapositions that human artists might never have imagined. Either way, AI-generated art forces us to reassess traditional notions of authorship and innovation.

AI-generated **music** follows a similar trajectory. Tools like **Amper Music**, **AIVA**, and **Jukebox** allow users to generate musical compositions based on genre, mood, tempo, or emotional tone. These systems model key aspects of music —melody, harmony, rhythm, instrumentation—and produce complete pieces that often demonstrate an impressive understanding of musical structure.

For composers and musicians, these tools offer significant value. They can help overcome creative blocks, spark new ideas, or provide starting points for original works. A composer might use AI to sketch out harmonic progressions, generate rhythmic variations, or simulate an unfamiliar musical style. While the AI doesn't bring human emotion or lived experience to the composition, it does expand the range of sonic possibilities available for exploration.

Yet, similar to AI art, AI-generated music also raises questions of originality and artistic value. Since these tools draw heavily from existing musical traditions, to what extent are their outputs new? The answer is complex. While the AI is informed by prior compositions, its ability to create novel combinations, unexpected harmonies, and imaginative blends of genre is undeniable. What it lacks in emotional depth, it compensates for with versatility and speed—qualities that, in the right hands, can lead to true artistic innovation.

Beyond aesthetic concerns, there are **ethical and legal questions** to consider. Chief among them is the issue of **copyright and authorship**. Who owns an AI-generated artwork or song—the user who provided the prompt, the developers of the algorithm, or someone else entirely? Legal systems around the world have yet to establish clear guidelines for intellectual property in the context of AI-generated content. This ambiguity can create complications for artists and developers alike, potentially limiting adoption or innovation due to uncertainty.

Bias is another important concern. If the AI is trained on biased datasets—images or music that reflect narrow cultural or societal perspectives—its outputs may unintentionally reproduce or reinforce harmful stereotypes. Preventing this requires careful dataset curation, ongoing testing, and ethical guardrails to ensure AI-generated content reflects diverse and inclusive perspectives.

Despite these concerns, the rise of AI-generated art and music does not diminish human creativity. On the contrary, it **augments it**. These tools provide artists with new materials, new methods, and new modes of expression. The key is to use them thoughtfully. Artists should see AI not as a stylistic shortcut, but as a collaborator—a way to explore uncharted creative territories, challenge their own boundaries, and experiment with fresh ideas.

The future of AI in the arts depends on **fostering a thoughtful, ethical, and human-centered approach**. This means:

- Prioritizing transparency in how AI tools are trained and used

- Developing clear authorship and copyright standards

- Investing in inclusive, diverse datasets

- Encouraging experimentation and artistic control

As AI continues to evolve, so too will our understanding of creativity itself. What counts as "original"? How do we define artistic intent in a collaborative system? What role does emotion play in art and music, and how can technology support or expand it?

These are not questions with easy answers—but they are questions worth asking. The partnership between human creativity and algorithmic ingenuity is not a threat. It is a **catalyst** for a new era of artistic exploration.

In this emerging landscape, the most powerful works will likely be those that combine the best of both worlds—human vision, emotion, and experience, enhanced by AI's ability to process, simulate, and generate at scale. By embracing this collaboration responsibly, we can create a future where art and music continue to evolve, reflecting not only who we are, but also what we can imagine together.

COPYRIGHT AND OWNERSHIP IN THE AGE OF AI: NAVIGATING LEGAL ISSUES

The rapid advancement of AI in creative fields has cast a spotlight on a pressing issue often overshadowed by the excitement of technological innovation: copyright and ownership. While AI continues to expand the possibilities of artistic and musical expression, the legal frameworks governing creative work were built for a world where only humans created art. As AI-generated content proliferates, fundamental questions arise: Who owns the rights to a digital painting generated by Midjourney? Is it the user who composed the prompt, the developers who created the tool, or, in a more abstract sense, the AI itself? These questions are not just theoretical, they have real consequences for creators, businesses, and the future of intellectual property law.

Copyright laws around the world generally recognize **human authorship** as a prerequisite for protection. They were designed to reward the originality and intention behind human-created works. AI tools, however, function differently. They rely on vast datasets of pre-existing content—art, music, writing—learning patterns, styles, and structures to produce novel outputs. This blurs the line between originality and derivation. Can something created without consciousness, emotion, or intent truly be called "authorship"?

In most jurisdictions, the answer remains no. AI-generated works typically **do not qualify for copyright protection** unless there is a clear human author guiding the creative process. This legal ambiguity leaves users and developers in a gray zone. If an AI-generated image strongly resembles a copyrighted work from its training data, could it be considered infringing? And who would bear the liability—the user, the AI's developers, or the original rights holders?

A commonly proposed solution is to **amend copyright laws** to account for AI-generated works. This could involve creating a new category of rights for works generated with minimal human input or granting ownership to the person who provided the prompts and parameters that shaped the final output. Such frameworks would need to strike a delicate balance—offering protection to encourage innovation while avoiding overreach that stifles creativity or unfairly benefits corporations at the expense of individual artists.

Another approach is the concept of **joint authorship**, where the human user and the AI system are seen as collaborators in the creative process. In theory, this would allocate rights proportionally based on the contributions of each party. However, in practice, quantifying the contribution of an algorithm is highly complex. Was the human simply selecting from AI-generated outputs? Or did they refine and build upon them in a meaningful way? The answers will differ case by case, making blanket rules difficult to apply.

A growing concern is the **copyright status of the training data** itself. AI systems are trained on enormous volumes of existing media—often without the consent of the original creators. If these models inadvertently replicate copyrighted material, it raises questions about whether the resulting work constitutes derivative content. Developers and platforms must consider how training data is sourced and whether usage complies with fair use, licensing, or ethical guidelines. Failing to address these issues could lead to widespread litigation and reputational risks.

Recent **legal cases** have begun to shape this debate. Courts have generally reaffirmed the principle that only human-made works are eligible for copyright protection. In 2023, for example, the U.S. Copyright Office reaffirmed that a piece generated entirely by an AI system cannot be copyrighted under current law unless there is meaningful human authorship involved. However, these rulings are only the beginning. As AI tools become more autonomous and more widely adopted, legal systems will be forced to revisit and refine their positions.

Beyond legal considerations, the **ethical implications** of AI-generated content deserve attention. Does widespread AI authorship dilute the value of human creativity? Does it reduce opportunities for artists, writers, and musicians to earn a living? These questions touch on core values related to originality, labor, and cultural expression. They also speak to broader social equity concerns: if powerful companies control the most advanced AI models, will they monopolize creativity itself?

One possible safeguard could involve **compensating original creators** whose work was used in training data, perhaps through licensing schemes or collective remuneration models. Another could involve mandating **transparency** in how AI models are trained and used, so users and consumers understand where content originates and what influences it.

As AI-generated content becomes more prevalent, the risk of **market saturation** with low-cost, machine-made media raises legitimate concerns about fairness. Human creators may find it harder to compete economically, even if their work is more meaningful or resonant. Policymakers will need to consider mechanisms that support and protect creative professionals, such as public funding for the arts, education in emerging creative technologies, or ethical guidelines for commercial AI deployment.

At present, the landscape remains unsettled. There is **no unified global approach**, and countries are moving at different speeds toward regulation. In the meantime, developers, users, and artists must navigate a legal terrain filled with uncertainty. What's clear is that the conversation around copyright and AI can no longer be deferred.

To ensure that AI continues to serve creativity rather than undermine it, we need **collaborative policymaking**, informed public debate, and ongoing dialogue among technologists, legal experts, artists, and cultural institutions. By reimagining copyright for a world that includes both human and machine creativity, we can foster a future where innovation thrives—ethically, sustainably, and inclusively.

AI AND THE FUTURE OF CREATIVITY: HUMAN–AI SYNERGIES

The previous discussion explored the complex legal and ethical issues surrounding AI-generated content. But beyond questions of ownership lies a more exciting prospect: the emergence of powerful creative synergies between humans and artificial intelligence. Rather than viewing AI as a rival, we should recognize it as a collaborator—one that expands our imagination and opens new frontiers for artistic expression.

Humans and AI possess fundamentally different, yet complementary, strengths. Human creators bring intuition, emotion, cultural context, and the depth of lived experience. We tell stories shaped by memory, identity, and personal meaning. These qualities give art its emotional resonance, turning brushstrokes, melodies, or words into deeply moving works.

AI, in contrast, excels at analyzing data, identifying patterns, and generating variations at remarkable scale and speed. It can process vast creative datasets, simulate thousands of design iterations, and propose novel combinations beyond what a single person might imagine alone. This is not competition—it's collaboration.

Picture a composer struggling with a section of a piece. An AI tool could generate dozens of harmonic options, offering textures the composer hadn't considered. Or an artist, exploring styles from surrealism to digital realism, could use AI to prototype visual ideas before committing to canvas. In these cases, the creator remains firmly in control. Refining, rejecting, and elevating what the AI suggests.

This symbiotic relationship is already transforming creative industries. In **music**, AI tools assist with composition, orchestration, and sound design. Composers use AI to break creative blocks, explore unfamiliar genres, and construct rich sonic landscapes. The outcome isn't machine-made music, it's **co-created** work that blends human emotion with computational experimentation.

In **visual art**, tools like **Midjourney** and **DALL·E 2** help artists generate striking images from simple text prompts. These tools serve as creative accelerators, enabling artists to explore stylistic options, brainstorm concepts, or craft fine details more efficiently. Far from replacing traditional skill, AI enhances it— freeing artists to focus on emotional impact, symbolism, and storytelling.

In **literature**, writers are using AI to assist with world-building, narrative design, and character development. AI helps authors brainstorm plotlines, generate draft text, and play with tone and voice. It's not about outsourcing authorship but enriching the creative process, providing writers with fresh perspectives and an endless well of inspiration.

Beyond these traditional creative fields, AI is reshaping **fashion design**, **architecture**, and **filmmaking**. Designers use AI to generate textile patterns and conceptual collections. Architects explore structural innovations guided by AI optimization. Filmmakers rely on AI for editing, animation, and visual effects

—allowing directors to focus more on storytelling and creative vision.

As this collaboration deepens, so too must our awareness of the challenges. **Bias in AI models**, shaped by the data on which they are trained, can skew artistic outputs and perpetuate stereotypes. **Ethical use of training data** and **algorithmic transparency** must become central to responsible creative practice. It's essential to develop tools that reflect diverse perspectives, and that creators are empowered to guide these tools with intentionality and integrity.

Another key concern is **access**. Today's most powerful creative AI tools are not universally available. Bridging this digital divide means expanding education, infrastructure, and policy support to ensure that creators around the world can benefit from AI's potential—regardless of geography or socioeconomic status.

It is also crucial to **preserve the central role of the human artist**. The fear that AI might replace human creativity is understandable but largely misplaced. The most impactful creative works resonate because of their humanity—because they reflect someone's inner world, values, and story. AI may provide tools, but humans shape meaning. The future of creativity lies not in automation but in **augmentation**.

To realize this vision, we must invest in:

- **Creative education** that incorporates AI literacy
- **Ethical guidelines** for training and deploying creative models
- **Legal frameworks** that recognize and reward human–AI collaboration
- **Platforms** that make AI tools accessible, intuitive, and inclusive

Imagine a future where AI not only generates suggestions

but also offers creative critique. Highlighting emotional tone, narrative pacing, or stylistic alignment. Or tools that adjust their responses based on the artist's mood, goals, or artistic values. The integration of AI and human creativity will only grow more fluid and responsive.

Ultimately, this is not a battle between humans and machines. It is a partnership. One in which human imagination is supported, not replaced, by artificial intelligence. This collaborative model has the potential to **elevate artistic innovation**, inspire cultural dialogue, and unlock expressions previously beyond our reach.

We are at the dawn of a new era in creativity—an era where technology and humanity harmonize. With thoughtful design, inclusive access, and a commitment to artistic integrity, we can shape a future where the full potential of both human and machine is realized.

PRACTICAL APPLICATIONS: USING AI TOOLS FOR CREATIVE PROJECTS

The potential of AI-powered creativity is exciting—but how do you actually use these tools to enhance your creative work? This chapter offers a hands-on guide to integrating AI into your creative process, navigating common challenges, and making the most of this evolving technology.

Choosing the Right Tool

The AI ecosystem is diverse and rapidly evolving, and selecting the right tool depends entirely on your discipline and objectives.

For **visual artists**, popular platforms include:

- **Midjourney**: Known for generating surreal, stylized imagery from text prompts.

- **DALL·E 2**: Offers more photorealistic results and greater control over image parameters.

- **Stable Diffusion**: Open-source and highly customizable, with strong community support.

- **NightCafe Creator**: A user-friendly platform ideal for beginners seeking quick results.

Each tool has its own strengths, and finding the best fit often comes down to personal preference, project goals, and experimentation.

For **musicians**, options include:

- **Amper Music**: Great for generating royalty-free music for media projects with a streamlined interface.

- **Jukebox (by OpenAI)**: Experimental and capable of generating original pieces in various styles.

- **AIVA**: Offers greater creative input, letting users tailor emotional tone, instrumentation, and style.

For **writers**, AI-powered assistants can help with idea generation, style refinement, and narrative development:

- **Jasper**: Ideal for marketing copy and short-form content.

- **Copy.ai**: A versatile tool that supports a wide range of writing tasks.

- **Sudowrite**: Geared toward creative writers, offering tools for character building, dialogue suggestions, and descriptive prose.

Integrating AI into Your Workflow

No matter which tool you choose, AI works best as a creative **collaborator**, not a replacement. To integrate AI effectively:

1. **Clarify your creative goals**: Are you looking to overcome writer's block, brainstorm visual ideas, or generate variations? Define your objective before engaging with the tool.

2. **Treat outputs as starting points**: Use AI-generated content as raw material. Your role as the artist is to curate, refine, and infuse the work with your personal voice.

3. **Iterate often**: Experimentation is key. Adjust your prompts, settings, or inputs to explore a variety of outputs.

Example 1: Graphic Design

Imagine you're creating a visual campaign for a coffee brand. Instead of sketching every concept by hand, you might use **Midjourney** with a prompt like:

"A steaming cup of coffee in an art deco café, warm colors, minimalist design, early morning sunlight."

The tool will generate several striking visuals, allowing you to choose the best concept and refine it using design software. This speeds up ideation and lets you focus on detail and messaging.

Example 2: Creative Writing

Suppose you're writing a historical novel but struggling to depict a particular scene. **Sudowrite** can suggest descriptive passages in varying tones and styles, offering fresh angles or phrases you might not have considered. You remain the author —choosing the best pieces and tailoring them to your narrative voice.

Example 3: Music Composition

A composer using **AIVA** to create a film score might input parameters like "uplifting," "orchestral," and "moderate tempo." The AI generates several melodies, and the composer selects the best elements, edits the arrangement, and layers in their unique stylistic touch. The final composition reflects both technological efficiency and human emotion.

Example 4: Fashion and Design

A fashion designer might use AI to generate textile patterns based on a theme—say, "organic geometry with neon accents." The tool quickly produces dozens of variations, offering a rich palette of ideas. The designer curates and customizes these patterns, weaving them into a larger collection.

Overcoming Challenges

1. **Bias in AI Models**: AI is trained on real-world data, which means it can inherit biases. Be vigilant about the content AI produces, and edit as necessary to avoid unintentional messaging or stereotypes.

2. **Managing Expectations**: AI is not a magic wand. While it can spark creativity and accelerate workflows, it doesn't eliminate the need for human oversight, intuition, and craftsmanship.

3. **Legal Considerations**: Ownership of AI-generated content varies by platform and jurisdiction. In most cases, users retain commercial rights, but it's essential to review the terms of service and seek legal counsel for high-profile or commercial projects.

4. **Accessibility and Inclusion**: Not all creators have equal access to high-performance AI tools. Bridging this digital divide requires education, open-source alternatives, and supportive infrastructure to ensure equity in creative innovation.

The Human Element

No matter how advanced AI becomes, the human element remains irreplaceable. AI may generate options, but it cannot replicate emotional nuance, lived experience, or the cultural context that human artists bring to their work. The most successful projects will result from thoughtful **collaboration**, where AI provides inspiration and assistance, and humans apply judgment, vision, and meaning.

Looking ahead, AI tools will become more intuitive, more responsive to creative intent, and potentially capable of offering **feedback and critique**, not just output. Imagine tools that help artists refine their work by suggesting improvements in tone, composition, or emotional impact.

The Future of Creative Collaboration

Embracing AI as a partner opens up new possibilities for storytelling, design, music, and more. By strategically integrating these tools into your process, you can unlock efficiency, broaden your creative palette, and push into unexplored territory.

The creative process is not being automated—it's being **amplified**. The future of art is not human versus machine, but human **with** machine: a partnership that promises to redefine what's possible.

ALGORITHMIC BIAS: IDENTIFYING AND MITIGATING UNFAIR OUTCOMES

Algorithmic bias is one of the most pressing ethical challenges in the age of artificial intelligence. It refers to systematic and repeatable errors in computer systems that produce unfair or discriminatory outcomes—often unintentionally. These biases are not typically the result of malicious design, but rather stem from the data used to train AI models. As the saying goes: **garbage in, garbage out**. If a machine learning model is taught to recognize cats using only images of fluffy white Persians, it may fail to identify a sleek black panther as a cat. This simple analogy illustrates a core principle of AI: algorithms learn what we teach them, and if that training data is biased or incomplete, the model's decisions will reflect those flaws.

The consequences of algorithmic bias can be serious, especially in sectors that directly impact people's lives—such as healthcare, finance, hiring, and criminal justice. In healthcare, for example, an AI system trained predominantly on data from one demographic group may misdiagnose or inadequately treat individuals from other groups, exacerbating disparities in care.

In lending, biased algorithms might systematically deny credit to applicants from underrepresented communities, reinforcing cycles of economic inequality. And in criminal justice, risk assessment tools have been shown to reflect—and even amplify—existing systemic biases, contributing to unequal treatment before the law.

One particularly well-documented case of algorithmic bias involves **facial recognition technology**. Numerous studies have found that these systems perform significantly better at identifying lighter-skinned individuals than those with darker skin tones. The root cause? Training datasets that are overwhelmingly composed of images of lighter-skinned people. As a result, the models struggle to accurately identify people from other demographic groups, with profound implications for law enforcement, border control, and public safety. In some instances, these flaws have led to **wrongful arrests**, highlighting the urgent need for reform and oversight.

Another important example is the use of AI in **hiring and recruitment**. Suppose a company deploys a machine learning algorithm to screen job applicants. If the system was trained on past hiring data that reflects a bias toward male candidates, it might learn to favor resumes that resemble those previously selected—regardless of actual qualifications. Even if gender isn't explicitly part of the data, the model may pick up on proxies, such as names or extracurricular activities. Without deliberate intervention, the result can be a **technologically reinforced form of discrimination**.

The dangers of unchecked algorithmic bias go beyond individual cases. They can create **systemic harm**, reducing access to opportunity, increasing inequality, and undermining trust in technology. The lack of transparency in many AI systems—often described as the "black box" problem—compounds this risk. If users and developers cannot explain how an algorithm arrives at a decision, it becomes nearly impossible to audit or challenge biased outcomes.

How Can We Address Algorithmic Bias?

Thankfully, there are several strategies to identify and mitigate bias in AI systems:

1. **Use Diverse and Representative Training Data**
   The most critical step is to ensure that the data used to train AI models accurately reflects the diversity of the real-world populations they affect. This means intentionally sourcing data from different demographics and contexts and ensuring that no single group is underrepresented or overrepresented. In some cases, this may require collecting new data to fill gaps in existing datasets.

2. **Conduct Rigorous Testing and Validation**
   Before deploying an AI model, it should be tested extensively on a variety of datasets—especially those that reflect the diversity of the intended user base. Testing should not only focus on accuracy, but also assess fairness, equity, and performance across demographic groups. Without this level of scrutiny, hidden biases can go unnoticed and cause long-term harm.

3. **Implement Ongoing Monitoring and Auditing**
   Bias isn't always static. AI systems can develop new biases over time as they are updated or exposed to fresh data. Continuous monitoring allows teams to identify problematic trends early and take corrective action. Regular audits by independent reviewers can also provide accountability and transparency.

4. **Apply Fairness-Aware Learning Techniques**
   A variety of technical methods exist to address bias

during model training. These include techniques like **sample reweighting**, **adversarial debiasing**, and **equalized odds adjustments**. The best approach often depends on the specific type of bias and the characteristics of the dataset and may require iterative testing and refinement.

5. **Improve Algorithm Transparency and Interpretability**
Developing models that are explainable and interpretable helps developers, stakeholders, and users understand how decisions are made. Transparency makes it easier to identify where bias may be creeping in—and to intervene before harm occurs.

6. **Involve Diverse and Interdisciplinary Teams**
Bias mitigation isn't just a technical problem. It's also social and ethical. Diverse teams, including technologists, ethicists, social scientists, and community representatives, bring a wider range of perspectives to the design and deployment of AI systems. This interdisciplinary collaboration helps surface assumptions and blind spots that might otherwise be overlooked.

Why It Matters

Fighting algorithmic bias is not a one-time fix—it's a **continuous process** that requires attention, resources, and a willingness to adapt. As AI becomes more embedded in our lives, its influence on justice, opportunity, and human dignity will only grow. The stakes are too high for inaction.

By adopting inclusive datasets, embedding fairness testing into every stage of development, and fostering transparency, we can work toward a future where AI not only avoids harm but actively contributes to a more equitable society. When wielded responsibly, AI has the potential to reduce bias and improve decision-making—but only if we remain committed to **designing with intention and accountability**.

PRIVACY AND SECURITY: PROTECTING DATA IN AN AI-DRIVEN WORLD

The rise of artificial intelligence has transformed how we collect, process, and use data—ushering in an era of unprecedented capability and complexity. While AI enables remarkable advancements in fields such as healthcare, finance, and education, it also raises serious concerns about **privacy** and **security**. As AI systems grow more powerful, the volume and sensitivity of personal data they handle increase dramatically, necessitating robust safeguards to protect individual rights in this increasingly data-driven world.

The Scope of Data Collection

One of the primary concerns in AI development is the **scale and scope of data collection**. To function effectively, AI systems often rely on vast datasets that include sensitive personal information—such as location data, health records, online browsing histories, financial transactions, and even biometric data. While this data is essential for training AI models and improving system performance, it introduces serious **risks of misuse, surveillance, and unauthorized access**.

Consider smart home devices. While they offer convenience, they also gather information about conversations, routines, and preferences. Similarly, fitness trackers and health apps collect intimate details that, if exposed, could affect employment, insurance, or personal safety. Even small data points, when aggregated, can paint a detailed picture of an individual—often without their knowledge or consent.

Facial Recognition and Surveillance

The deployment of **facial recognition technology** is another area of heightened concern. Widely used in public surveillance and law enforcement, these systems can track individuals without their awareness. This raises serious ethical dilemmas around **informed consent, accuracy, and the potential for bias**, particularly when studies show that many facial recognition systems perform significantly worse on individuals with darker skin tones. The lack of transparency in how these systems are implemented adds another layer of risk.

Cybersecurity Vulnerabilities

AI systems are also **vulnerable to cyberattacks**. As they process and store large volumes of personal data, they become prime targets for hackers seeking to exploit this information. Breaches can lead to identity theft, financial fraud, reputational harm, and even manipulation of AI outputs. For example, malicious actors could manipulate content moderation tools, alter medical diagnostics, or disrupt financial decision-making systems. The growing sophistication of cyber threats requires **continuous improvements to AI system security**, including encryption, anomaly detection, and secure data storage.

Regulatory Frameworks

To combat these risks, regulatory frameworks like the **General Data Protection Regulation (GDPR)** in the European Union and the **California Consumer Privacy Act (CCPA)** in the United

States have emerged as critical tools. These laws aim to:

- Empower users with greater control over their personal data

- Enforce transparency in data collection and usage

- Hold organizations accountable for data misuse or breaches

However, technology is evolving faster than legislation. Current regulations, while foundational, often struggle to keep up with the pace of innovation. This calls for ongoing policy refinement, international cooperation, and proactive industry engagement.

Best Practices for Safeguarding Data

Protecting personal data in an AI context requires a **multi-layered strategy**:

1. **Data Minimization**
   AI systems should collect only the data necessary for their function. Adopting a "need-to-know" approach limits exposure and reduces the risk of unnecessary data misuse.

2. **Security by Design**
   Incorporating robust security measures into the architecture of AI systems is essential. This includes encryption, multi-factor authentication, role-based access control, and regular security audits.

3. **Transparency and Explainability**
   Clear, accessible privacy policies and the development of **explainable AI (XAI)** systems help users understand how their data is used and how AI decisions are made.

4. **User Consent and Control**
   Users should provide **informed, unambiguous**

consent for data collection and retain the right to withdraw that consent. Interfaces should make it easy to manage privacy preferences.

5. **Anonymization and Pseudonymization**
   Where possible, personal identifiers should be removed or masked. These techniques reduce the risk of re-identification if data is compromised.

6. **Incident Response and Breach Management**
   Even with precautions, data breaches may occur. Organizations must have a clear **response plan** that includes detection, containment, mitigation, and prompt notification to affected individuals.

7. **Culture of Data Ethics**
   Organizations must embed **privacy and ethical AI principles** into their operations. This includes staff training, internal audits, and clear accountability for data protection at every level.

Building Public Trust

Ultimately, privacy and security are not just technical concerns, they are **foundational to public trust**. When people understand how their data is used, when they feel they have control, and when organizations act transparently, trust is built. That trust is essential for the continued advancement and adoption of AI technologies.

Looking Forward

As AI continues to evolve, so too must our frameworks for managing its risks. A collaborative approach is key. Developers must design with privacy in mind. Policymakers must draft adaptive, forward-looking regulations. And individuals must stay informed, empowered to make decisions about their digital lives.

The future of AI hinges on our ability to **balance innovation with integrity**. Privacy and security must be guiding principles —not afterthoughts. Only then can we build a future where artificial intelligence enhances our lives without compromising our rights.

TRANSPARENCY AND EXPLAINABILITY: UNDERSTANDING HOW AI SYSTEMS WORK

As AI systems become increasingly embedded in our daily lives, the demand for **transparency** and **explainability** has never been more urgent. While artificial intelligence offers tremendous benefits, processing vast datasets, identifying patterns, and making rapid decisions. It Often does so through complex models whose inner workings remain opaque to most users. This so-called **"black box" problem** introduces serious ethical and practical challenges, particularly when AI is used in high-stakes contexts like healthcare, criminal justice, or finance.

Imagine a loan application denied by an AI-powered system. The applicant naturally wants to know why. Without an explanation, the decision feels arbitrary or even discriminatory. This lack of transparency can erode trust, inhibit accountability, and obscure potential bias or error.

Why Transparency Matters

Transparency is not just a desirable feature—it is a **core requirement for responsible AI development**. When people cannot understand how an AI system arrives at its conclusions, it becomes difficult to:

- Evaluate the fairness of the decision
- Identify and correct errors or biases
- Build user trust in the technology
- Ensure accountability in legal or regulatory contexts

In short, an AI system that cannot be understood cannot be trusted, and trust is foundational to ethical AI deployment.

The Complexity of Explainability

Achieving explainability in AI is challenging for several reasons:

1. **Model Complexity**
   Modern AI models, particularly deep learning neural networks, contain millions (or even billions) of parameters. These systems often discover patterns in data that humans cannot easily trace or interpret, making it difficult to explain specific outputs in simple terms.

2. **Bias in Training Data**
   AI systems learn from the data they are fed. If the training data contains biases—such as underrepresentation of certain groups—those biases can be encoded into the system's decision-making. For example, a facial recognition tool trained primarily on lighter-skinned individuals may underperform when identifying people with darker skin tones.

3. **Opaque Algorithms**
   Some algorithms do not lend themselves easily

to introspection. While decision trees and linear models can be relatively transparent, deep learning systems operate more abstractly. Understanding what a model has learned often requires specialized tools and interpretation techniques.

Strategies for Greater Explainability

Despite these hurdles, significant progress is being made through both **technical and procedural solutions**:

- **Explainable AI (XAI)**
  XAI refers to techniques that help demystify AI models by offering **visualizations, textual justifications**, or simplified models that approximate complex systems. These methods can highlight which features most influenced a decision, or even provide step-by-step logic trails that users and auditors can follow.

- **Interpretable Models**
  When possible, using simpler models—such as decision trees or logistic regression—can improve interpretability without sacrificing too much accuracy. While not suitable for every task, they are valuable in situations where **transparency is paramount**, such as in healthcare or finance.

- **Modular Design**
  Designing AI systems with **modular architectures** can help isolate specific decision-making steps, making it easier to identify where and how a result was derived. This approach allows each component to be analyzed and improved independently.

- **Data Transparency**
  Understanding an AI system's behavior also requires transparency in its **training data**. Clear

documentation of how data was collected, cleaned, and labeled helps uncover potential biases and supports efforts to improve fairness.

- **Model Documentation and Reporting**
  Techniques like model cards and datasheets for datasets provide **standardized, accessible summaries** of a model's capabilities, limitations, and intended uses—promoting responsible development and deployment.

Building Trust and Accountability

Explainability is central to **building public trust**. Users are more likely to adopt and support AI systems when they understand how decisions are made, especially when those decisions directly affect them. In industries such as insurance, employment, and criminal justice, the absence of clear reasoning behind AI outputs can lead to widespread skepticism, legal challenges, and reputational damage.

Transparency is also essential for **accountability**. If an AI system makes a mistake, stakeholders need to be able to determine what went wrong, who is responsible, and how the issue can be corrected. Without explainability, tracing errors or biases becomes exceedingly difficult, impeding justice and regulatory oversight.

The Challenge of Trade-Offs

It's important to acknowledge that **greater explainability can sometimes come at the cost of performance**. Simplifying a complex model for the sake of clarity may reduce its predictive accuracy. The key lies in finding the **right balance**—developing tools that offer both strong performance and meaningful insight. This is a major area of current AI research and innovation.

Looking Forward: A Human-Centric Approach

The future of ethical AI depends on continued investment in transparency and explainability—not just at the technical level, but within broader organizational and societal frameworks. This includes:

- Training developers and designers to prioritize interpretability

- Engaging ethicists, regulators, and impacted communities in the design process

- Encouraging interdisciplinary collaboration between data scientists, social scientists, and legal professionals

In the long term, **explainability should not be an afterthought**, but a **built-in requirement** of any AI system that affects people's lives in meaningful ways.

Conclusion

The path forward requires a shared commitment to **clarity, accountability, and human oversight**. As AI becomes more powerful and pervasive, understanding how these systems work —and ensuring they reflect human values—will be essential for ensuring their ethical use. The black box must give way to transparency. By demystifying AI, we not only foster trust and adoption, but also empower people to question, improve, and guide these technologies toward **fairer, more inclusive outcomes**.

ACCOUNTABILITY AND RESPONSIBILITY: WHO IS RESPONSIBLE WHEN AI MAKES MISTAKES

The previous chapter explored the importance of transparency and explainability in AI systems. Yet even the clearest explanation of how an AI system works doesn't answer the most pressing question when something goes wrong: **who is responsible**? This is the growing challenge of accountability in the age of artificial intelligence.

From self-driving car accidents to biased hiring algorithms and misdiagnosed medical cases, the complexity of modern AI systems makes assigning responsibility anything but straightforward. Unlike traditional technologies, AI often operates through intricate webs of data, algorithms, and human involvement, creating a legal and ethical maze when failures occur.

A Case Study in Complexity: Self-Driving Cars

Imagine a self-driving car is involved in a collision. Is the fault with the software engineers who developed the algorithm? The hardware manufacturers who supplied the faulty sensors? The human "safety driver" who failed to intervene in time? Or perhaps the car made the best decision it could in an impossible situation?

These aren't hypothetical questions. Real-world cases have already shown how difficult it is to attribute blame in AI-driven incidents. Determining fault often requires extensive forensic analysis, multidisciplinary investigations, and legal review. The result is often lengthy litigation, blurred liability, and, at times, reduced public confidence in emerging technologies.

High Stakes Beyond the Road

Similar complexity arises in healthcare. Suppose an AI diagnostic tool incorrectly labels a serious illness as benign, delaying essential treatment. Should the developers be held accountable for the algorithm's misjudgment? Or is it the hospital's responsibility for relying on an imperfect tool? What about the physician who made the final decision based on the AI's recommendation?

Even more ethically fraught are AI applications in **criminal justice**. Risk assessment algorithms used to predict recidivism have been shown to replicate racial and socioeconomic biases present in historical data. If a defendant is denied bail or receives a longer sentence based on a flawed algorithm, **who bears responsibility**? The developers? The court that used the system? Or the policymakers who approved its implementation?

Each actor plays a role, but our current legal systems often lack the nuance to assign responsibility clearly or fairly.

The Legal and Ethical Gap

One of the primary issues is that **existing laws were not designed for AI**. Most legal systems assume human intention, negligence, or direct action—criteria difficult to apply to autonomous systems. Developers, manufacturers, deployers, and users may each play a part, but the chain of accountability is often unclear.

This legal ambiguity has real-world consequences:

- **Companies may delay adoption** of beneficial AI technologies out of fear of liability.

- **Developers may hesitate** to innovate or release new tools without clear risk protections.

- **Victims of AI errors may struggle** to seek redress or hold the right parties accountable.

Without legal clarity, public trust erodes, and the potential benefits of AI may go unrealized.

Building a Framework for AI Responsibility

To address these challenges, a **multi-faceted approach** is needed:

1. **Define Responsibility in the AI Context**
   Legal definitions must evolve to account for AI's distributed decision-making. Some jurisdictions are exploring the concept of "algorithmic accountability" or adapting product liability law to better reflect AI's complexities. This might involve creating legal distinctions for **"AI deployers," "AI developers," and "AI operators."**

2. **Assign Role-Based Accountability**
   Responsibility should align with **roles and actions** within the AI lifecycle. Developers may be responsible for ensuring technical accuracy, while organizations deploying the AI may be accountable for oversight, transparency, and ethical use.

3. **Standardize Auditing and Oversight**

AI systems should undergo **independent audits**, just as financial institutions are regularly assessed for compliance and accuracy. These audits should evaluate fairness, bias, reliability, and real-world performance. Reporting requirements could make it easier to detect risks early.

4. **Create and Enforce AI-Specific Regulations**
   Regulatory frameworks should address:
   - Data governance and privacy
   - Algorithmic transparency
   - Incident reporting and remediation
   - Redress mechanisms for those harmed by AI International cooperation is crucial here. Without cross-border consistency, companies may engage in **regulatory arbitrage**, moving operations to countries with looser oversight.

5. **Establish AI Incident Response Protocols**
   When AI systems cause harm, affected parties should know **what recourse exists**. Just as companies must disclose data breaches, there should be requirements for disclosing serious AI failures and taking corrective action.

6. **Promote Interdisciplinary Collaboration**
   Technologists, ethicists, legal scholars, business leaders, and civil society organizations must work together to develop policies that reflect **technical realities and social values**. Ethical AI is not only a technical challenge—it's a societal one.

Trust Requires Accountability

Without clear paths to accountability, AI-related mistakes can cause long-term harm not just to individuals, but to public confidence in the technology itself. Ensuring trust in AI means building systems where responsibilities are clearly defined, oversight is robust, and redress is possible when harm occurs.

Ultimately, accountability is about more than assigning blame. It's about building systems that respect human rights, uphold fairness, and **earn the trust of those they serve**.

Conclusion

As artificial intelligence becomes more embedded in critical sectors, we must face a pivotal question: what happens when things go wrong? Answering that question requires **rethinking legal frameworks**, clarifying roles, and embedding accountability into the very fabric of AI development.

This challenge won't be solved overnight. But through proactive policymaking, transparent design, and a commitment to ethical principles, we can ensure that AI not only performs well—but also upholds the standards of fairness, responsibility, and justice that society expects.

BUILDING TRUST IN AI: PROMOTING ETHICAL AI DEVELOPMENT AND DEPLOYMENT

Building trust in artificial intelligence is not merely a technological challenge, it is a societal imperative. The transformative potential of AI spans nearly every sector, from healthcare and finance to education and public safety. But realizing these benefits depends on addressing fundamental ethical concerns and ensuring responsible development and deployment. This requires a comprehensive, life-cycle approach that begins with data collection and extends through continuous system monitoring.

Fairness and Bias Mitigation

A foundational pillar of ethical AI is **fairness**. AI systems learn from data, and when that data reflects existing social biases— whether racial, gender-based, or socioeconomic—the AI is likely to replicate and even exacerbate those biases. For example, facial recognition systems have been found to exhibit higher error rates when identifying individuals with darker skin tones, a result of training data that lacks adequate demographic representation.

This underscores the urgent need for:

- Diverse, inclusive, and representative training datasets

- Rigorous pre-deployment testing

- Ongoing validation and auditing across demographic groups

Bias doesn't end once a model is launched. Continuous updates, feedback, and auditing are essential to identify and correct emerging issues over time. Transparency in both data sourcing and algorithmic design is also critical to allow for independent scrutiny and foster public accountability.

Privacy Protection and Data Ethics

Another cornerstone of AI trust is **data privacy**. Many AI systems rely on large volumes of personal information, ranging from GPS location data and browsing history to health records and biometric identifiers. This introduces serious risks regarding misuse, surveillance, and data breaches.

Ethical AI development must prioritize:

- Robust data governance frameworks

- Adherence to laws such as the GDPR (Europe) and CCPA (California)

- Anonymization and differential privacy to protect identities

- Clear mechanisms for obtaining informed consent and enabling data control

The principle of **data minimization**—collecting only what is strictly necessary for a given purpose—should be a guiding standard.

Explainability and Transparency

Trust in AI is severely undermined when users cannot understand how decisions are made. Many AI systems, especially deep learning models, operate as "black boxes," obscuring their decision-making logic. This lack of explainability is especially concerning in high-stakes domains like credit scoring, hiring, and criminal justice.

Explainable AI (XAI) aims to address this challenge by offering tools that:

- Visualize key decision factors
- Highlight influential data inputs
- Provide human-readable summaries of algorithmic decisions

Although full transparency in complex models remains elusive, incremental improvements in explainability are possible—and necessary—to build user confidence and regulatory compliance.

Accountability and Legal Responsibility

Trust is impossible without **accountability**. When AI systems cause harm—whether through biased outcomes, unsafe behavior, or misinformation—clear mechanisms must exist to assign responsibility and pursue redress.

Building this accountability involves:

- Establishing legal frameworks tailored to AI's unique risks
- Clarifying the roles of developers, deployers, and end-users
- Creating pathways for impacted individuals to seek remediation

- Developing independent oversight bodies to audit AI systems

International collaboration is essential to prevent regulatory loopholes and ensure consistency across borders.

Education, Culture, and Public Engagement

Promoting ethical AI also requires **broad public engagement** and **organizational alignment**. Educating both technical professionals and general audiences about AI's capabilities, risks, and ethical dimensions helps build societal resilience.

Strategies include:

- Integrating AI ethics into STEM education
- Hosting public forums on emerging technologies
- Offering corporate training for developers and managers on responsible AI
- Encouraging whistleblower protections and internal ethics channels

Within organizations, a culture of responsibility must be cultivated. This includes ethical review boards, diversity in development teams, and ethical risk assessments alongside traditional testing protocols.

Continuous Monitoring and Feedback Loops

AI systems evolve over time. They adapt to new inputs and environments, which makes **ongoing monitoring** vital. Initial fairness or accuracy at launch does not guarantee sustained performance.

Effective trust-building requires:

- Feedback loops involving users and stakeholders
- Post-deployment audits

- Mechanisms for tracking real-world impacts

- Adaptive updates aligned with ethical benchmarks

Responsible AI development is not a one-time event, but a **continuous, iterative process** involving learning, refinement, and reevaluation.

Conclusion

Building trust in AI demands more than technical excellence. It requires an integrated approach grounded in fairness, privacy, transparency, accountability, public engagement, and vigilant monitoring. By embedding ethical principles across the entire AI lifecycle, we can ensure that AI is not only powerful but also **trustworthy, inclusive, and aligned with human values**.

This is not a finish line to be crossed. It is a **long-term commitment**—a journey of collaboration between technologists, policymakers, communities, and users—to ensure that AI becomes a force for good in society.

THE SPREAD OF MISINFORMATION: HOW AI EXACERBATES THE PROBLEM

The rapid advancement of artificial intelligence has ushered in an era of unprecedented technological capabilities. Yet, it has also created new avenues for manipulation and deception. Among the most significant challenges AI presents is its potential to **exacerbate the spread of misinformation**. The ease with which AI can generate realistic yet fabricated content—combined with the speed and reach of digital platforms—has created a perfect storm for the proliferation of fake news and deepfakes, blurring the lines between reality and fiction.

AI-generated misinformation stems from a confluence of powerful technologies. Advanced models, accessible through online platforms and user-friendly interfaces, now allow users to generate **realistic images, videos, and audio clips**. Known as **deepfakes**, these outputs can convincingly depict individuals saying or doing things they never actually did. What was once the domain of highly technical experts is now within reach of individuals with minimal expertise, expanding the risk of misuse.

AI's influence is not limited to visual media. **Natural Language Processing (NLP)** models can craft compelling fake news articles, blog posts, or social media content designed to **manipulate public opinion**. These texts are often grammatically flawless, emotionally resonant, and contextually plausible. Making them difficult for the average reader to discern as inauthentic. These models can exploit cognitive biases, tailoring messages to specific demographics to maximize their psychological impact.

The architecture of the internet, and especially social media, intensifies this issue. Engagement-driven algorithms **reward sensational content**, inadvertently boosting the visibility of misleading information. When AI-generated misinformation aligns with emotionally charged topics, it can **go viral**, reaching millions before fact-checkers can respond. The result is a **feedback loop**: misinformation spreads quickly, is shared widely, and becomes increasingly difficult to correct once it takes hold.

Real-World Consequences

The implications are both broad and serious. Misinformation:

- **Undermines trust** in democratic institutions, media, and scientific authorities

- Fuels **social division**, often aligning with polarizing narratives

- **Compromises public safety**, especially during health crises like pandemics

- Affects **election outcomes** by manipulating voter perception through doctored media or fabricated quotes

Recent incidents have illustrated the dangers. Deepfakes of public figures making inflammatory remarks, AI-generated health advice promoting pseudoscience, and fake news stories seeded by bots are no longer rare outliers—they are symptoms of a new information ecosystem that AI helps power.

Combating AI-Generated Misinformation

Technology-based solutions are evolving rapidly. Researchers are developing AI models to detect manipulated content—an arms race between **misinformation generation** and **detection**. Deepfake detection tools analyze inconsistencies in pixels, lighting, blinking rates, and audio sync. In parallel, digital watermarking and content authentication protocols (such as Adobe's **Content Authenticity Initiative**) aim to validate the provenance of digital content.

However, **technology alone is insufficient**. A comprehensive response must include:

1. Media Literacy and Public Education

Empowering individuals to critically evaluate sources is essential. Media literacy campaigns can:

- Teach how to spot AI-generated content
- Promote skepticism of sensational headlines
- Explain the tactics used in misinformation campaigns

Education should also extend to **journalists, educators, and policymakers**, helping them recognize and respond to misinformation more effectively.

2. Platform Accountability

Social media and content-sharing platforms must:

- Invest in robust detection and removal systems
- Demote or label potentially misleading content

- Partner with fact-checkers and researchers to develop best practices
  Companies have a responsibility to balance free speech with the ethical imperative to prevent harm.

3. Policy and Regulation

Governments can play a role by:

- Crafting laws that address the creation and malicious distribution of deepfakes

- Supporting transparency in political advertising and campaign content

- Funding public interest research on misinformation
  These policies must be **technologically informed**, adaptable, and crafted with input from civil society to ensure they don't stifle legitimate expression.

4. Cross-Sector Collaboration

Solving this problem requires cooperation between:

- **Tech companies**, who control the tools

- **Governments**, who legislate

- **Educators**, who train media-savvy citizens

- **Civil society organizations**, who research and advocate for ethical tech

The Road Ahead

The fight against AI-generated misinformation is ongoing and urgent. While detection tools and policy responses continue to improve, **awareness and education remain our first line of defense**. Ignoring the threat of AI-powered misinformation would risk deepening mistrust in institutions and exacerbating divisions already present in society.

By fostering a culture of critical thinking, supporting ethical AI development, and building cross-sector alliances, we can **protect the integrity of public discourse**. The challenge is significant—but so is the opportunity to shape a digital future where truth can still thrive.

IDENTIFYING AI-GENERATED MISINFORMATION: TOOLS AND TECHNIQUES

The ability of AI to generate increasingly realistic misinformation presents a significant challenge—but fortunately, a growing arsenal of tools and techniques is emerging to help us detect and counteract these fabrications. While no method is foolproof, especially as generative technologies rapidly advance, these approaches represent crucial first steps in the broader effort to stem the spread of fake news and deepfakes.

One of the most promising methods for detecting manipulated images and videos is **metadata analysis**. Metadata, often invisible to casual users, contains essential details about how and when a digital file was created or modified. This includes information like the file's creation date, device model, software used, and more. Inconsistencies in this metadata can signal potential manipulation. For example, a video claimed to be from 2020 might show metadata indicating a 2023 creation date, immediately raising red flags. Although sophisticated actors may attempt to erase or forge metadata, many automated tools are now capable of identifying anomalies, giving investigators and journalists a valuable means of verifying authenticity.

Beyond metadata, **forensic analysis of visual and audio elements** can reveal the subtle fingerprints of AI manipulation. Deepfakes, for instance, may contain visual artifacts such as inconsistent lighting, unnatural blinking, or distortion around the mouth and eyes. These discrepancies are often imperceptible to the human eye but detectable by specialized detection algorithms. Similarly, AI-generated voice recordings can be scrutinized for unusual inflection patterns, inconsistencies in tone or pitch, and deviations from a speaker's known vocal signature. As detection tools evolve, they are becoming increasingly adept at spotting these inconsistencies—even as generative models improve in realism.

Another key strategy involves **narrative and linguistic analysis**. While large language models can produce grammatically sound and stylistically fluent text, they still struggle with deep coherence, emotional nuance, and logical consistency. AI-generated stories or news articles may feature implausible timelines, superficial emotional depth, or overly generic phrasing. In more technical or journalistic content, fabricated sources or unverified claims can be telltale signs. Scrutinizing the structure, logic, and sourcing of a narrative, especially if it appears designed to provoke strong emotional reactions, can help uncover signs of automated authorship.

Fact-checking platforms are another critical line of defense. Websites such as Snopes, PolitiFact, and FactCheck.org maintain extensive databases of verified claims. While they don't detect AI use directly, they help verify the *content* of claims—whether AI-generated or not. Newer AI-driven fact-checking tools are also emerging that cross-reference large bodies of trusted sources to evaluate the plausibility of real-time content. When paired with user diligence, these tools significantly increase the chances of identifying misinformation before it spreads.

A deeper layer of analysis involves examining **social media context**. Many misinformation campaigns rely on coordinated activity, often using bots or fake accounts to artificially amplify certain narratives. Patterns such as rapid reposting, identical messaging across accounts, or unnatural spikes in engagement can signal inauthentic behavior. Social media monitoring tools are increasingly able to map these networks and flag suspicious content distribution patterns.

In tandem with technological approaches, developing **critical thinking and media literacy** remains fundamental. Individuals must learn to ask key questions: Who created this content? What is its source? Are there other perspectives? What evidence supports it? Media literacy training, especially in schools and public education campaigns, helps foster a healthy skepticism that resists manipulation without veering into cynicism. The goal is not to mistrust all information but a **measured, analytical approach to evaluating it**.

Another emerging defense mechanism is **digital watermarking**. This technique embeds invisible identifiers into audio, image, or video content to verify its authenticity and trace its origin. While watermarking isn't yet standardized across platforms, initiatives like the **Content Authenticity Initiative (CAI)** and **C2PA (Coalition for Content Provenance and Authenticity)** aim to implement industry-wide solutions. These approaches offer promising infrastructure to distinguish real content from synthetic manipulations and maintain the integrity of original media.

Ultimately, identifying AI-generated misinformation requires a **layered approach**, combining technological tools with human judgment. Whether it's analyzing metadata, detecting visual or linguistic inconsistencies, consulting fact-checking resources, or evaluating the credibility of information based on its dissemination patterns, the tools exist—but they must be used consistently and responsibly.

As AI-generated misinformation becomes more sophisticated, our defenses must evolve accordingly. This demands continuous investment in **research and education**, collaboration between tech companies and civil society, and robust policy frameworks that support transparency and accountability in content creation and distribution. By strengthening detection methods and promoting critical media engagement, we can build a more resilient society—one better equipped to navigate the complexities of the modern information landscape.

COMBATING THE SPREAD OF MISINFORMATION: STRATEGIES AND SOLUTIONS

The fight against AI-generated misinformation is not solely a technological battle; it is a multifaceted challenge that demands a coordinated response from social media platforms, educators, policymakers, and individuals. As primary vectors for the dissemination of false or misleading content, social media platforms bear a significant responsibility in mitigating the spread of misinformation. While algorithmic content moderation is improving, these systems remain imperfect. One of the most critical needs is **greater transparency in how platform algorithms function**—specifically, how they prioritize and amplify content. Without understanding these mechanisms, it's difficult to assess how misinformation is being inadvertently boosted or inadequately filtered.

To effectively address this issue, platforms must **invest in advanced detection tools**, capable of identifying deepfakes and other synthetic media designed to mislead. These tools should evolve in tandem with the techniques used by malicious actors, ensuring platforms can respond to emerging threats in real time. However, technology alone is not enough. Platforms must also implement **user-centric systems** for reporting misinformation, making it easy for individuals to flag suspicious content and receive timely feedback on their reports. Transparent, responsive moderation practices enhance user trust and foster community engagement in the battle against false information.

Effective communication strategies are just as crucial as technological tools. Platforms should **regularly engage with their user base**, clearly articulating their policies, the limitations of current technologies, and the steps being taken to combat misinformation. Partnering with researchers, fact-checkers, and civil society organizations can amplify these efforts and build a shared understanding of evolving threats. Public awareness campaigns, educational content, and real-time updates about major misinformation trends can help users stay vigilant and informed.

Education remains one of the most powerful long-term solutions. **Media literacy programs** must be integrated into school curricula at all levels, starting in early education. These programs should go beyond basic research skills, focusing instead on developing **critical thinking abilities** and a deeper understanding of how and why misinformation spreads. Students should learn to evaluate sources, identify emotional manipulation, recognize logical fallacies, and question unsupported claims. Interactive learning, real-world case studies, and scenario-based training can make this education practical and impactful.

In addition to student education, teachers must be equipped to **navigate and teach in the digital information environment**. This includes recognizing signs of manipulated content, guiding students through nuanced discussions about bias, and modeling responsible digital behavior. As misinformation tactics evolve, education systems must remain agile and update their materials and methods accordingly. Encouraging a mindset of inquiry—not cynicism—is key to helping students become discerning consumers of information.

The role of policymakers is equally critical. Governments must walk a fine line: **safeguarding freedom of expression while protecting the public from demonstrably false and harmful content**. Rather than engaging in censorship, legislation should focus on **promoting transparency and accountability** among digital platforms. This might include mandating algorithmic disclosures, requiring platforms to maintain moderation logs, and establishing content reporting standards.

Laws addressing the malicious use of deepfakes are especially needed. Legislation should criminalize the intentional creation and distribution of synthetic media for defamation, manipulation, or fraud—while also ensuring that genuine creative and journalistic uses of AI are not unduly restricted. To strike this balance, policymakers should collaborate closely with **technologists, ethicists, and civil liberties advocates**, ensuring that emerging rules are both effective and respectful of rights.

Governments also have a vital role in **funding research and innovation**. Supporting the development of cutting-edge detection tools, advancing AI explainability, and fostering public-private partnerships are essential to building robust defenses. Funding should extend to both academic institutions and industry, encouraging cross-sector innovation in areas such as real-time deepfake detection, content watermarking, and misinformation attribution.

Ultimately, success will depend on **broad-based collaboration**. Social media companies, educators, researchers, and governments must align around a shared vision: an informed society where truth can withstand the pressures of manipulation. Coordinated efforts should focus on **developing common standards**, encouraging the exchange of best practices, and creating **global frameworks** that address misinformation as a borderless threat. Open communication channels and sustained investment in both people and technology are critical.

The rise of AI-generated misinformation is not a temporary problem. It is a defining challenge of the digital era. To confront it effectively, we must cultivate a **culture of media literacy, civic responsibility, and technological resilience**. The future of truth in the public square depends not just on smarter algorithms, but on a society equipped to question, verify, and hold the digital world accountable.

THE ROLE OF AI IN DETECTING MISINFORMATION: LEVERAGING TECHNOLOGY AGAINST ITSELF

The irony is hard to miss: the same artificial intelligence technologies capable of generating deepfakes, fake news, and synthetic media are also being used to combat them. This paradox lies at the heart of one of the most urgent information challenges of our time—detecting and mitigating AI-generated misinformation before it spreads. As AI-driven content becomes increasingly difficult to distinguish from authentic material, researchers and companies are developing advanced AI tools to fight deception with precision and scale.

AI's greatest strength in this fight lies in its capacity to analyze massive volumes of digital content far beyond human capabilities. Every day, millions of images, videos, and posts are uploaded across platforms, making manual moderation unrealistic. AI systems, trained on both authentic and manipulated content, can flag suspicious items by analyzing patterns, inconsistencies, and metadata anomalies that may indicate fabrication.

One of the most effective AI-based strategies is the use of computer vision tools to detect deepfakes. **Reality Defender**, a leading real-time deepfake detection platform, uses neural networks to examine facial inconsistencies, blinking patterns, unnatural transitions, and pixel-level artifacts. Its browser extension can flag altered content before users consume it—an important frontline defense for journalists, businesses, and government agencies alike.

Similarly, **Sensity AI** specializes in detecting visual threats like manipulated videos and facial morphing. Their platform is often used by newsrooms and law enforcement agencies to monitor malicious synthetic media and identify potential threats early. Sensity's deep learning engine provides both detection and context, highlighting the specific manipulation method used and the likelihood of tampering.

In the realm of verifying image authenticity, **Truepic** provides a suite of tools that focus on **provenance and media integrity**. Rather than detecting fakes after they are made, Truepic emphasizes **content verification at the point of capture**. Their Truepic Lens technology embeds tamper-proof metadata —including timestamps, GPS data, and device signatures—into images and videos, offering a cryptographic trail that confirms whether content has been altered.

When it comes to text-based misinformation, natural language processing (NLP) models are proving essential. AI tools like **Grover** (developed by the Allen Institute for AI) and **GPTZero** (developed to detect AI-authored text) use language patterns, sentence structure, and stylistic cues to evaluate the authenticity of written content. These systems analyze markers like repetition, lack of source attribution, and unnatural phrasing—common characteristics of AI-generated or misleading narratives.

Still, the success of detection models depends heavily on the quality and diversity of their training datasets. A system trained on only one form of disinformation (e.g., political deepfakes in English) may fail to identify misinformation in other languages or domains. As a result, detection systems must be continually updated to reflect the evolving tactics used by bad actors—an approach that requires adaptability, collaboration, and global-scale data collection.

Importantly, many of these systems now go beyond binary flags of "true" or "false." Modern tools increasingly provide **contextual intelligence**—explaining *why* something is flagged, citing inconsistencies or referencing conflicting information. This is critical for building public trust. For example, **Microsoft's Content Credentials** (in partnership with Adobe and the Content Authenticity Initiative) allows platforms to embed visible and invisible watermarks into authentic content. When altered media is detected, the system compares the current file to the original version, giving users transparency into what changes occurred and when.

Despite the progress, challenges remain. The misinformation landscape is rapidly evolving. AI-generated content is becoming more sophisticated, leveraging adversarial techniques specifically designed to evade detection. As AI detection systems improve, so too do the methods used to bypass them. Creating an ongoing arms race.

There are also ethical considerations to weigh. AI detection tools can inherit bias from their training data, potentially over-policing some types of content or disproportionately flagging material from underrepresented communities. To counteract this, developers must prioritize transparency, diversity in training data, and regular audits to avoid misuse or unintended censorship.

Moreover, while detection technology is necessary, it is not sufficient on its own. AI must be integrated into a **broader misinformation defense strategy** that includes media literacy, platform accountability, and public education. Fact-checking organizations like **PolitiFact**, **Snopes**, and **Full Fact** now use AI to cross-reference viral claims with verified sources in real-time. Combined with AI-powered detection, these tools allow users to make informed decisions quickly and confidently.

Looking ahead, AI tools are being designed not only to detect misinformation but to **disarm it at scale**—with automatic labeling, source verification, and proactive moderation. In many cases, AI-generated detection systems can respond faster than human fact-checkers and offer more consistent performance across languages, topics, and formats.

Still, no algorithm can fully replace human judgment. AI should be viewed as a **co-pilot**, not a gatekeeper—augmenting human oversight with scalable, high-speed analysis. The most promising path forward involves **hybrid systems** that combine the speed of AI with the discernment and contextual awareness of trained human moderators.

In conclusion, AI's role in detecting misinformation is both powerful and essential. With tools like Reality Defender, Truepic, and Sensity leading the charge, the technology exists to defend the information ecosystem from synthetic content and coordinated deception. But technology alone won't solve the problem. Success depends on a shared commitment to transparency, ethical design, global collaboration, and public trust. As AI evolves, so must our strategies, ensuring that truth remains visible in a digital landscape increasingly clouded by falsehoods.

FUTURE CHALLENGES AND OPPORTUNITIES: THE ONGOING ARMS RACE AGAINST MISINFORMATION

The battle against misinformation has evolved into a high-stakes arms race—one that is constantly escalating in speed, complexity, and global impact. Artificial intelligence, while an essential tool in identifying and flagging false information, is also the driving force behind increasingly sophisticated misinformation tactics. This duality creates a relentless cycle of innovation and counter-innovation, where defenders and adversaries race to outmaneuver each other with every advancement.

The Speed, Scale, and Sophistication of Misinformation

One of the most daunting challenges in this ongoing struggle is the sheer velocity at which misinformation spreads. Social media algorithms, optimized for engagement, often amplify sensationalist content—regardless of its truthfulness. In a matter of hours, false narratives can reach millions of users, long before fact-checkers or moderation teams have time to intervene. Compounding this problem is the use of AI-powered bots and fake accounts that can rapidly generate and disseminate coordinated waves of misleading content, overwhelming human response systems.

Today's misinformation is no longer confined to crude clickbait or poorly Photoshopped memes. Generative AI tools like **StyleGAN**, **Runway ML**, and **ElevenLabs** are enabling the creation of hyper-realistic deepfakes and synthetic audio with astonishing ease. These manipulated assets can portray public figures saying or doing things they never did, influencing elections, eroding reputations, or stoking social unrest.

The Adaptation Problem: Innovation on Both Sides

As detection tools evolve, so do the strategies of misinformation actors. Adversaries are constantly testing the boundaries of detection systems, using adversarial AI techniques to create deepfakes that evade forensic scrutiny. This cat-and-mouse game requires defenders to adopt a mindset of constant evolution. Tools like **Reality Defender**, **Sensity AI**, and **Deepware Scanner** are leading the charge, employing computer vision and machine learning to uncover visual anomalies, inconsistent lighting, or temporal discrepancies in videos and images. Yet even these state-of-the-art tools must be updated regularly to remain effective.

Moreover, AI-powered systems themselves are not immune to bias. If detection algorithms are trained on skewed datasets or built without transparency, they may inadvertently suppress legitimate content or amplify existing inequalities. Maintaining fairness and accountability requires rigorous audits, inclusive training data, and ethical oversight at every stage of AI development.

The Human Element: Media Literacy and Education

Technology alone cannot win this fight. A critical weakness in society's defenses is the lack of widespread media literacy. Many individuals are unprepared to evaluate the credibility of the content they encounter online. Misinformation thrives when people fail to question what they read, see, or hear.

The solution lies in education. Media literacy programs must be embedded into school curricula starting at the elementary level, teaching students how to verify sources, recognize manipulation, and evaluate information critically. Tools like **Checkology** and **NewsGuard** already provide interactive lessons and browser extensions to help users assess source reliability. When paired with AI-assisted platforms like **Logically Facts** or **ClaimBuster**, these educational tools can provide real-time feedback, creating an ecosystem that blends learning with action.

The Legal and Regulatory Frontier

As misinformation becomes more international, so too must the response. While nations like Germany have enacted regulations like the **NetzDG** to hold platforms accountable for removing harmful content, enforcement remains challenging on a global scale. The internet knows no borders, and neither does AI-generated misinformation.

Governments must develop consistent international frameworks that balance freedom of expression with public safety. This involves regulating the malicious use of deepfakes, requiring transparency in algorithmic design, and incentivizing technology companies to adopt robust verification systems. Proposed policies like the **EU AI Act** and ongoing efforts by organizations like the **Partnership on AI** reflect the urgency of crafting responsible and enforceable governance.

Opportunities on the Horizon: Tech for Truth

Despite the obstacles, significant opportunities exist to turn the tide. AI is making measurable progress in real-time content verification. Tools like **Truepic Lens** are embedding cryptographic signatures and metadata at the point of capture, enabling instant authentication of images and videos. Paired with blockchain technology, these signatures could soon offer immutable provenance for digital content, creating a tamper-proof audit trail.

Fact-checking organizations are also leveraging AI to scale their reach. **Full Fact**, for example, uses AI-driven monitoring to scan broadcast transcripts and flag misleading claims for human review. Similarly, **Google's Fact Check Explorer** and **Facebook's CrowdTangle** provide searchable databases and trend analysis to help journalists and citizens trace viral misinformation back to its origins.

Meanwhile, startups like **Hive Moderation** and **ActiveFence** are helping content platforms automate the moderation of misinformation at scale, freeing up human moderators to focus on the gray areas where AI still struggles.

The Path Forward: Collaboration, Not Competition

Ultimately, defeating misinformation requires a hybrid model—one that integrates the speed and scale of artificial intelligence with the discernment and contextual judgment of human experts. A multi-pronged approach must include:

- Continued investment in AI-powered detection and forensic tools.

- Universal integration of media literacy programs.

- Transparent legal frameworks to guide ethical AI use.

- Cross-sector collaboration among governments, platforms, and civil society.

- Platforms offering clearer user feedback and algorithm transparency.

The real victory in this arms race won't come from building the most advanced detection algorithm or the flashiest fact-checking tool. It will come from a shared societal commitment to truth, critical thinking, and responsible digital citizenship. Technology may be the frontline, but people remain the heart of this fight.

By fusing innovation with education, policy, and public trust, we can create an information ecosystem where truth not only survives—but thrives.

THE PROMISE OF AUTOMATION: INCREASED EFFICIENCY AND PRODUCTIVITY

The promise of automation, powered by rapid advancements in artificial intelligence (AI), is a transformative force reshaping industries and economies around the globe. At its core, AI-driven automation delivers a powerful combination of speed, precision, and adaptability—boosting efficiency, driving productivity, and opening doors to unprecedented economic growth. But the true potential of automation lies not merely in replacing human labor, but in augmenting human capabilities, streamlining processes, and optimizing resource allocation to achieve greater output with fewer inputs.

Transforming Manufacturing with Precision and Speed

Nowhere is the impact of automation more apparent than in the manufacturing sector. Industrial robots, enhanced by computer vision and deep learning, can perform welding, assembly, and painting tasks with unmatched consistency and precision. Companies like **ABB**, **Fanuc**, and **KUKA Robotics** have pioneered robotic solutions that reduce waste, minimize defects, and increase production speed. In the automotive industry, Tesla and BMW have integrated such automation to streamline assembly lines, cut production costs, and increase throughput without compromising quality.

Boosting Service Sector Productivity with AI

Automation is also revolutionizing the service industry. Customer service chatbots, powered by natural language processing (NLP) tools like **LivePerson**, **Ada**, and **Google Dialogflow**, are capable of resolving a wide range of customer queries in real time. These AI-driven agents reduce wait times, lower operational costs, and improve user satisfaction by allowing human representatives to focus on high-complexity tasks. Banks like Bank of America (with its AI assistant **Erica**) and telecom providers like Vodafone are already deploying such technologies to scale their customer service operations efficiently.

Driving Innovation in Healthcare

The healthcare sector stands to benefit significantly from automation. AI tools like **PathAI** and **Aidoc** can analyze X-rays, MRIs, and CT scans with remarkable accuracy, assisting radiologists in identifying abnormalities such as tumors or hemorrhages earlier than traditional methods. Robotic-assisted surgery platforms like **Intuitive Surgical's da Vinci system** enable minimally invasive procedures with higher precision, reducing recovery times and improving outcomes. As AI becomes more deeply integrated into diagnostics and treatment planning, it holds the promise of more personalized and effective patient care.

Revolutionizing Logistics and Supply Chain Management

AI-powered automation is also transforming logistics. Companies such as **Amazon, FedEx**, and **DHL** leverage predictive analytics and route optimization algorithms to improve delivery accuracy and reduce transportation costs. Tools like **ClearMetal** and **FourKites** offer real-time supply chain visibility, enabling companies to anticipate delays, optimize inventory levels, and meet customer demand with greater reliability.

Enabling Sustainable Agriculture

In agriculture, AI-driven automation is helping farmers address labor shortages and climate variability. Drones and AI-powered platforms like **Blue River Technology** and **John Deere's See & Spray** systems enable precision agriculture by monitoring crop health, optimizing fertilizer and pesticide use, and improving yield predictions. These innovations not only increase productivity but also reduce environmental impact— a vital consideration in addressing global food security and sustainability goals.

Challenges: Job Displacement and Workforce Readiness

Despite these benefits, AI-driven automation raises critical concerns—chief among them, job displacement. As machines take over repetitive or manual tasks, certain roles may become obsolete, particularly in manufacturing, logistics, and administrative functions. According to a 2023 report by the **World Economic Forum**, automation could displace 85 million jobs by 2025—but it may also create 97 million new roles, particularly in data analysis, machine learning, and human-AI collaboration.

To navigate this transition, governments and businesses must invest in upskilling and reskilling initiatives. Programs like **Coursera for Government, IBM SkillsBuild**, and **Google Career Certificates** are helping workers prepare for emerging roles in AI, cloud computing, and digital operations. The goal should not be to resist automation, but to prepare people to thrive alongside it.

Ethical Considerations and Human Oversight

Automation must also be approached with an ethical lens. AI algorithms are only as fair as the data they are trained on. Without careful attention, automation systems—especially in hiring, lending, or law enforcement—can perpetuate systemic bias. Tools like **Fairlearn** and **IBM's AI Fairness 360 Toolkit** are designed to detect and mitigate bias in AI models, while organizations like the **AI Now Institute** advocate for greater transparency and accountability in automation design.

Moreover, human oversight remains essential. While AI can handle many tasks autonomously, human judgment is needed in edge cases, ethical dilemmas, and mission-critical decisions. This is especially true in sectors like healthcare, criminal justice, and finance, where the consequences of algorithmic errors can be life-altering.

Conclusion: Toward a Collaborative Future

AI-driven automation holds enormous promise for accelerating productivity, reducing costs, and improving service quality across industries. However, realizing its full potential requires a balanced approach. One that embraces technological innovation while addressing economic, ethical, and social implications.

Rather than framing AI as a threat to human workers, we must shift the narrative to one of partnership. AI should augment human strengths, not replace them. By fostering collaboration between machines and people, we can unlock new possibilities for innovation and creativity.

To ensure an equitable transition, stakeholders—governments, businesses, educators, and communities—must work together to invest in training, build inclusive AI systems, and prioritize human-centric design. In doing so, we can build a future where automation is not just efficient, but empowering—a catalyst for progress that benefits all.

THE RISKS OF AUTOMATION: JOB DISPLACEMENT AND ECONOMIC INEQUALITY

The rosy picture of increased efficiency and productivity painted by AI-driven automation needs a crucial counterpoint: the very real risks of widespread job displacement and the exacerbation of economic inequality. While automation promises a brighter future for some, it casts a long shadow over the livelihoods of many others, demanding a careful and proactive response from governments, businesses, and individuals alike. The challenge is not to halt technological progress but to manage its impact to ensure a just and equitable transition.

One of the most immediate concerns is the displacement of workers. As AI-powered systems grow increasingly capable of performing tasks once requiring human intelligence, entire job categories are at risk. This isn't a theoretical worry—it's already happening in numerous industries. The manufacturing sector, for example, has experienced significant job losses due to the widespread adoption of robotics and automated assembly lines. While productivity has soared, many workers have found themselves without the skills or opportunities needed to adapt to this new reality.

This trend isn't confined to manual labor. Even traditionally white-collar roles are increasingly vulnerable. Data entry clerks, administrative assistants, paralegals, and financial analysts are now encountering competition from AI-powered tools capable of handling large volumes of information, automating reporting, and even generating insights. As language models and process automation improve, the scope of potential disruption continues to expand.

The transportation industry offers a particularly stark illustration. The rise of autonomous vehicles promises to revolutionize logistics and mobility, but it also threatens the jobs of millions of truck drivers, taxi operators, and delivery personnel. While new jobs may emerge in the autonomous vehicle ecosystem, such as in maintenance, system monitoring, or fleet analytics, the skills required are vastly different from those used in driving, making the transition anything but seamless.

The ripple effects of job displacement extend to entire communities. Regions economically dependent on a single industry or employer, such as factory towns or logistics hubs, are particularly vulnerable. Mass layoffs in these areas can trigger a cascade of secondary impacts: shuttered small businesses, declining home values, and reduced funding for schools and public services. Without targeted intervention, these communities face long-term economic and social decline.

While some argue that automation will ultimately create more jobs than it eliminates, this optimistic outlook often overlooks the scale of the skills gap. Many of the new jobs created in AI development, robotics, and digital infrastructure require advanced technical expertise. Workers displaced from roles like assembly line manufacturing or long-haul trucking may not have the time, resources, or support needed to retrain for these emerging roles.

Bridging this skills gap requires coordinated investment in education and workforce development. Retraining programs should focus not only on technical competencies like coding or data analysis but also on transferable soft skills—such as communication, critical thinking, and adaptability—that will remain valuable in an AI-augmented economy. Governments, employers, and educational institutions must collaborate to align training efforts with the demands of the modern workforce.

Just as automation increases productivity, it also concentrates wealth. Businesses benefit from reduced labor costs, improved operational efficiency, and scalable digital systems, but those financial gains are often absorbed by shareholders and executives. Meanwhile, displaced workers face declining incomes, job insecurity, and limited upward mobility. This widening gap between those who profit from automation and those who are left behind fuels social inequality and economic polarization.

To address these structural imbalances, policymakers must explore bold and inclusive solutions. Proposals such as universal basic income (UBI), expanded unemployment insurance, and wage subsidies could provide financial stability for workers navigating economic transitions. Progressive taxation and wealth redistribution mechanisms could ensure that the gains of automation are shared more broadly across society. Stronger labor protections and collective bargaining rights would give workers more leverage in an increasingly automated economy.

The conversation about automation must evolve. It's not just a technical discussion—it's a social one. We need to move beyond a narrative of inevitability and embrace one of intentionality.

The future of work is not predetermined by code or algorithms, it's shaped by policy, education, and collective will. It's our responsibility to ensure that the benefits of innovation do not come at the expense of equity and human dignity.

A just transition to an AI-driven economy demands a holistic approach. This includes investments in inclusive education and retraining, strong safety nets, ethical governance of technology, and mechanisms to ensure that prosperity is shared. The goal is not to resist innovation but to harness it in ways that uplift rather than displace.

Automation should be a tool for empowerment, not exclusion. If managed wisely, it can reduce drudgery, boost creativity, and open new avenues for economic growth. But if left unchecked, it risks deepening divides and weakening the social fabric. The decisions we make today will shape whether AI becomes a driver of inclusion, or of inequality. The stakes could not be higher.

MITIGATING THE RISKS: STRATEGIES FOR A JUST TRANSITION

The transition to an AI-driven economy presents a critical challenge: how to embrace the transformative power of automation while mitigating its potentially disruptive impact on employment and economic inequality. The goal is not to halt progress but to ensure that its benefits are distributed broadly, not concentrated among a privileged few. This requires a proactive, coordinated response rooted in fairness and social responsibility. At the heart of this effort is the concept of a "just transition" a framework designed to manage the social and economic consequences of technological change, ensuring no one is left behind.

A key pillar of this transition is substantial investment in education and reskilling. The jobs emerging in an AI-enabled future often require fundamentally different skills than those of the past. While automation is expected to displace many workers in manufacturing, retail, administration, and logistics, it will also create new roles in fields like AI development, cybersecurity, data science, and clean energy infrastructure.

Meeting this shift head-on means governments, industries, and academic institutions must work together to close the growing skills gap.

Retraining programs must go beyond surface-level digital skills. They should cultivate transferable capabilities such as analytical thinking, collaboration, emotional intelligence, and communication. Skills that will remain valuable even as technology evolves. These programs should also reflect the realities of today's workforce, offering flexible, inclusive, and accessible learning pathways that meet people where they are. Support must be particularly strong for vulnerable populations: older workers facing industry collapse, women reentering the workforce, and historically marginalized communities that have long been excluded from high-growth sectors.

Social safety nets play a vital role in cushioning the impact of economic disruption. A universal basic income (UBI), for instance, could provide financial security for individuals during periods of job loss or retraining. Pilot programs in Finland and Stockton, California, have shown promising outcomes, including increased job-seeking activity and improved mental health. Other supports—such as expanded unemployment benefits, health care portability, and housing assistance—are equally important for navigating periods of instability.

Yet financial support alone is insufficient without addressing how economic gains from automation are distributed. Progressive taxation can help rebalance wealth by ensuring that the individuals and corporations benefiting most from AI advancements contribute fairly to the social contract. These revenues can then fund education, public infrastructure, and research. Additionally, strengthening labor rights—such as guaranteeing a living wage, expanding paid leave, and supporting collective bargaining—ensures workers retain power and dignity in the changing landscape of work.

A just transition also requires deep attention to the ethical use of AI systems, particularly in addressing algorithmic bias and discrimination. Without proper oversight, AI can reinforce systemic inequalities in hiring, lending, policing, and more. The data used to train AI often reflects historical injustices, which can lead to automated decisions that replicate human prejudice.

To counter this, we must embed **algorithmic ethics** into every stage of AI development and deployment. International frameworks like the **OECD Principles on AI** emphasize human-centered values, transparency, and accountability. The **European Union's AI Act** goes further by proposing risk-based regulations for AI applications, particularly in high-stakes sectors such as law enforcement and healthcare.

Research institutions like the **AI Now Institute** are helping define what responsible AI governance looks like in practice. Their work advocates for algorithmic audits, impact assessments, and stronger public accountability. Meanwhile, technical tools such as **IBM's AI Fairness 360** toolkit or Google's **What-If Tool** are enabling developers to test and refine their models to reduce discrimination.

To ensure AI is truly fair and inclusive, organizations must conduct independent audits, require transparency in model design and training data, and establish public channels for recourse when algorithms cause harm. These accountability mechanisms must be built into the legal and regulatory fabric, not simply left to corporate discretion.

As the structure of work evolves, we must also rethink employment models. Non-traditional work, such as freelancing, part-time roles, and gig labor, is becoming more common. These arrangements require policy adaptations to guarantee fair pay, access to benefits, and legal protections. Portable benefits schemes and digital labor rights initiatives are steps in the right direction, ensuring that all workers—regardless of classification

—are protected.

Examples from around the world highlight successful efforts in managing this transition. Singapore's **SkillsFuture** initiative provides residents with training credits to pursue upskilling throughout their lives. Germany's dual education system, combining apprenticeships with classroom learning, offers a strong model for integrating training with real-world job needs. Canada has supported laid-off workers with wage subsidies and wraparound services during major industrial transitions. These approaches demonstrate the value of proactive, people-centered policy.

Policy recommendations for a just transition include:

- **Expanding reskilling and upskilling programs**
  Partnering with industry to align training with labor market needs and ensuring programs are accessible, flexible, and inclusive.

- **Strengthening social safety nets**
  Supporting income continuity during retraining or job transitions through UBI, unemployment insurance, and healthcare access.

- **Reinforcing labor protections**
  Guaranteeing minimum wages, workplace rights, and legal protections for all workers, including those in the gig economy.

- **Implementing progressive taxation**
  Redirecting automation-driven gains to fund inclusive infrastructure, education, and health systems.

- **Embedding algorithmic ethics**
  Mandating independent audits, bias testing, transparency protocols, and accountability standards for all high-impact AI systems.

- **Building cross-sector partnerships**
  Encouraging collaboration between governments, employers, and educators to anticipate labor market shifts and co-create solutions.

The transition to an AI-powered economy is not only a technological journey, it's a deeply human one. Navigating this transition successfully will require foresight, empathy, and collaboration across every layer of society. While the risks are real, so are the opportunities to build a more resilient, equitable, and dynamic future of work.

Ultimately, a just transition ensures that automation serves people—not the other way around. With the right investments and ethical commitments, we can create a world where progress doesn't mean displacement, but empowerment. The future is still ours to shape.

AUTOMATION AND SOCIETY: RETHINKING WORK AND THE FUTURE OF LABOR

The previous discussion focused on mitigating the negative impacts of automation on employment and ensuring a just transition. However, the societal implications of widespread automation extend far beyond job displacement. The very nature of work, our understanding of productivity, and the structure of modern economies are all ripe for transformation —and this shift demands thoughtful, broad-reaching conversation.

One crucial aspect to consider is the impact of automation on work-life balance. While automation promises increased productivity, it also risks eroding the boundaries between professional and personal life. The "always-on" culture, driven by digital tools and the expectation of constant availability, already strains workers across industries. Automation, if not carefully managed, could exacerbate this challenge. Remote work offers autonomy and flexibility, yet it can also lead to extended work hours and the dissolution of personal time. Policies that protect against overwork, such as limits on after-hours communication and mandatory disconnection periods, are necessary to preserve employee well-being.

Beyond the question of balance, the nature of work itself is shifting. The traditional concept of long-term employment with benefits and a clear trajectory is giving way to a more fragmented labor market. The rise of the gig economy, characterized by short-term, task-based work, presents opportunities for flexibility but also introduces instability and a lack of essential protections. In this new reality, it is imperative to redesign labor frameworks to ensure that gig workers have access to healthcare, unemployment support, and retirement options, regardless of their employment classification.

As AI advances, it will also create entirely new categories of work, many of which are difficult to envision today. This shift demands an equally radical transformation of education. Curricula must evolve to prioritize creativity, critical thinking, emotional intelligence, and adaptability. A future-ready workforce is one equipped not just with technical skills but with the mindset to learn continuously.

Automation may also reshape economic organization itself. As barriers to entry fall and digital tools become more accessible, we may see a shift away from large, centralized corporations toward more decentralized models of work—freelancers, micro-businesses, cooperatives, and platform-based collectives. This new landscape will require updated regulatory frameworks and tax structures to ensure equity and fair contribution. It is not enough to celebrate efficiency; we must ensure it serves the broader public interest.

This transformation also demands ethical reflection. One critical concern is inequality. If the financial gains of automation flow primarily to a small elite, while the risks fall on vulnerable workers, the result will be deepening divides in wealth, opportunity, and social cohesion. Addressing this requires bold, redistributive policies, such as universal basic income, progressive taxation, and strong public investment in infrastructure and education.

Another equally pressing concern is the effect of automation on human dignity and identity. For many, work provides a sense of purpose and belonging. As machines take over routine and cognitive tasks, society must grapple with how to preserve meaning in life beyond employment. What does it mean to live a fulfilling life in a post-work economy? This is not just an economic question, it's a cultural and philosophical one.

Social cohesion is also at stake. Automation may reduce the daily interactions that workforces naturally provide, increasing isolation and diminishing a sense of community. Proactively fostering environments for human connection—through public spaces, civic engagement, and supportive technologies—will be key to maintaining social well-being.

Algorithmic ethics play a central role in this evolving world of work. As AI systems increasingly influence decisions in hiring, promotion, and task allocation, we must ensure they do not reinforce bias or discrimination. This calls for robust standards in fairness, transparency, and accountability. Algorithmic decisions must be auditable and explainable. Developers should follow ethical frameworks during the design phase—conducting impact assessments, involving diverse stakeholders, and ensuring ongoing oversight.

The path forward requires a collective, intentional effort:

- **Reimagine education** to foster lifelong learning, creativity, and resilience.

- **Protect flexible workers** with benefits and legal protections suited for non-traditional arrangements.

- **Invest in inclusive economic models** that distribute

gains from automation more equitably.

- **Develop algorithmic governance standards** rooted in fairness, explainability, and human oversight.

- **Cultivate civic dialogue** that includes all sectors of society—workers, technologists, ethicists, and policymakers.

The automation of work is not simply a technological phenomenon, it is a cultural and moral moment. We are being asked to decide what kind of society we want to build with the tools we've created. This future will not emerge by default. It must be shaped with intention, empathy, and a shared vision that places human dignity at its core.

CASE STUDIES: AUTOMATION SUCCESSES AND FAILURES

The transition to an AI-driven economy is fraught with both immense potential and significant peril. Understanding this dynamic requires examining real-world examples—the successes and failures of automation projects across diverse sectors. Analyzing these case studies reveals that successful automation hinges not only on technological feasibility but also on strategic planning, ethical foresight, workforce adaptation, and ongoing monitoring and adjustment.

One compelling example of successful automation is found in the manufacturing sector. Companies like Toyota, renowned for their lean manufacturing principles, have long integrated robotics and automated systems into their assembly lines. Their success stems not just from technological investment but from a holistic approach that includes meticulous planning, robust employee training, and a philosophy of continuous improvement. Rather than displacing workers, Toyota has re-skilled its workforce to collaborate with automation—managing, maintaining, and optimizing robotic systems—

thus creating higher-skilled, better-compensated roles. Data analytics is central to their iterative process, identifying inefficiencies and refining automation strategies to maximize productivity, product quality, and workplace safety.

In contrast, not all manufacturing automation projects have succeeded. Some companies have rushed to adopt robotic systems without sufficient planning or workforce integration, resulting in decreased productivity and higher operational costs. Lack of compatibility with existing systems and underestimating the training required to manage new technologies have often led to project delays and budget overruns. In these cases, sidelining human expertise and undervaluing organizational readiness have proven to be costly errors.

The service sector also illustrates both the promise and pitfalls of automation. Many organizations have adopted AI-powered chatbots and virtual assistants to streamline customer service operations. When implemented with user experience in mind, these systems improve efficiency and customer satisfaction. Companies that succeed in this space often employ a hybrid model. Where AI handles routine inquiries, and human agents tackle complex cases. These firms focus on conversational design and seamless transitions between human and automated support.

However, poorly designed chatbot deployments have backfired. When bots are unable to understand queries or escalate to human representatives, frustration builds quickly, damaging brand perception. These failures underscore the need for a user-centered design philosophy in customer-facing automation, prioritizing empathy and clear communication as much as operational efficiency.

In the financial sector, algorithmic trading has revolutionized how markets operate. High-frequency trading platforms powered by AI now execute trades in milliseconds. However, events like the 2010 Flash Crash—where the Dow Jones Industrial Average plunged nearly 1,000 points in minutes before rebounding, illustrate the potential dangers of unchecked automation. While the cause was traced to a combination of automated orders and insufficient safeguards, the incident prompted greater regulatory oversight and the development of circuit breakers to stabilize markets. Today, successful trading firms pair AI with human oversight, combining speed with prudent risk management.

Healthcare offers some of the most transformative and ethically sensitive applications of automation. AI is now used to analyze medical imaging, assist in surgical procedures, and support diagnostics. For instance, platforms like IBM Watson Health and Google's DeepMind have shown promise in assisting radiologists and pathologists. When rigorously tested and validated, these tools enhance accuracy and efficiency. However, failed deployments, where systems were inadequately vetted or produced biased outcomes, reveal the high stakes of automation in healthcare. Ethical concerns around data privacy, patient consent, and bias in training datasets remain central and require constant vigilance.

Agriculture has also seen notable innovation through AI. Precision agriculture systems leverage drones, satellite imagery, and machine learning to optimize irrigation, pesticide use, and crop monitoring. Companies like John Deere and startups such as CropX have delivered measurable gains in yield and sustainability. Yet, challenges persist when tools are not tailored to local environmental conditions or when training for farmers is inadequate. The lesson here is that technological solutions must be developed in partnership with end users, respecting local knowledge and fostering usability.

Across all these sectors, one pattern is clear: successful automation is not simply a matter of deploying advanced tools.

Success is shaped by:

- Strategic planning and phased implementation
- Inclusive workforce training and adaptation
- Transparent evaluation and ethical safeguards
- Collaboration among stakeholders
- A culture of continuous feedback and improvement

Failures, on the other hand, are often rooted in treating automation as a turnkey solution—overlooking the socio-technical context in which it operates. Neglecting the human element, whether in design, training, or execution, remains a persistent pitfall.

The overarching insight from these case studies is that automation's promise cannot be fulfilled by technology alone. Its success is equally dependent on leadership foresight, ethical stewardship, and the capacity to build systems that enhance human capabilities rather than replace them outright. As we continue to navigate this AI-powered transformation, it is our collective responsibility to ensure that automation enhances human well-being, advances equity, and sustains long-term economic resilience.

CHATGPT: MASTERING THE ART OF CONVERSATIONAL AI

ChatGPT, and similar conversational AI models, represent a significant leap forward in human-computer interaction. Moving beyond simple keyword searches, these tools engage in dynamic, context-aware conversations, offering a far more intuitive and productive way to interact with information and technology.

Mastering the art of leveraging ChatGPT effectively involves understanding its capabilities, limitations, and best practices for prompt engineering. This understanding empowers users to unlock the full potential of this powerful technology, transforming how they approach tasks ranging from creative writing to complex research.

One of the most immediate applications of ChatGPT is in content creation. Whether you need to generate marketing copy, draft emails, write blog posts, or create fictional narratives, ChatGPT can significantly accelerate your workflow. Its ability to adapt to various writing styles and tones makes it a versatile tool for diverse content needs. For instance, requesting a product description for a new smartwatch can yield a concise, compelling piece ready for immediate use. Similarly, asking for a humorous short story in the style of Roald Dahl will produce a surprisingly creative and engaging narrative. The key to success lies in crafting clear and specific prompts. Rather than a vague request like "write a story," a more effective prompt would be: "Write a short, humorous story about a mischievous robot dog who accidentally sends a flock of sheep into space, in the style of Roald Dahl." The level of detail in your prompt directly correlates with the quality and relevance of the output.

While this chapter focuses primarily on ChatGPT, it's worth noting that it exists within a broader ecosystem of conversational AI tools. Competitors such as Anthropic's Claude, Google's Gemini, and Microsoft's Copilot (built on OpenAI models) offer similar capabilities with different design philosophies and strengths. For example, Claude is often praised for its alignment with ethical constraints and safety, while Gemini emphasizes tight integration with Google's suite of products. Understanding the similarities and differences between these tools can help users choose the best platform for their specific needs.

Beyond creative writing, ChatGPT excels at answering questions and providing information. Its vast knowledge base, trained on a large dataset of text and code, enables it to respond to a wide range of inquiries. However, it is crucial to critically evaluate its responses. ChatGPT does not possess real-world understanding; it generates answers based on patterns learned from training data. For this reason, verifying information with multiple reliable sources is always advisable, especially when dealing with factual claims or sensitive topics. For example, asking ChatGPT about the history of the Roman Empire will yield a reasonably detailed summary, but cross-referencing this information with academic sources ensures accuracy and avoids potential misinterpretation.

Specifying your desired response format also matters. Requesting a concise summary or a detailed explanation can significantly affect the structure and depth of the answer.

Research assistance is another area where ChatGPT excels. It can summarize long documents, extract key information, or help generate research questions. Imagine needing to synthesize data from ten research papers on a specific topic. Rather than manually combing through each, you can feed the abstracts to ChatGPT and ask for a cohesive summary, saving significant time. Still, it's best viewed as a research assistant, not a replacement for rigorous scholarship. Any output should be verified and supplemented with primary sources to ensure validity. ChatGPT's strength lies in organizing complex data and offering accessible overviews, but it cannot judge credibility or context in the way a human researcher can.

In education, ChatGPT offers potential as a tool for enhancing learning. Students can use it to generate essay prompts, practice writing, and receive preliminary feedback. Teachers can generate customized lesson plans and learning activities tailored to their students' needs. However, this integration must be approached thoughtfully. It's essential that students learn to assess and critique the AI's output rather than accept it as definitive. The goal should be to supplement human instruction, not replace it, with AI-powered tools that promote critical thinking and engagement.

ChatGPT can also serve as a powerful assistant in programming. It can generate code snippets in various programming languages, help troubleshoot bugs or explain unfamiliar algorithms. For instance, asking ChatGPT to write a Python function to sort a list or to describe how a merge sort works can yield immediate, useful results. For junior developers and seasoned engineers alike, this can dramatically accelerate problem-solving. However, all code should be tested, reviewed, and understood before implementation. While ChatGPT may generate syntactically correct solutions, it does not guarantee optimized or secure code.

The effectiveness of ChatGPT hinges on prompt engineering. Clear, well-defined prompts result in far more accurate and useful responses than vague or ambiguous ones. For example, instead of asking "write about dogs," try: "Write a 500-word essay comparing the physical and behavioral traits of German Shepherds and Golden Retrievers." Providing context, constraints, and structure helps the AI deliver a more focused output.

Equally important is understanding ChatGPT's limitations. It does not generate original thought, nor does it possess common sense or lived experience. While it may produce convincing and articulate responses, it can also generate factually incorrect or logically inconsistent outputs. This makes regular verification essential. Always review AI-generated content for accuracy and suitability before using it in a professional or public context.

In conclusion, mastering ChatGPT requires a balanced understanding of both its strengths and limitations. When used thoughtfully, ChatGPT can serve as a valuable partner in writing, research, education, and coding. It is not a replacement for human insight, creativity, or judgment—but it can augment them in powerful ways. The key is to approach it as a tool that enhances, not substitutes, human intelligence. By developing effective prompt strategies, critically engaging with its responses, and applying human oversight, we can unlock new levels of productivity and creativity across countless fields. The journey to mastering conversational AI is ultimately a journey of collaborative problem-solving, one that invites us to think more deeply about how we learn, create, and communicate in a rapidly evolving digital world.

MIDJOURNEY: UNLEASHING YOUR INNER ARTIST WITH AI IMAGE GENERATION

Midjourney, along with other tools in the fast-evolving field of AI image generation, represents a thrilling democratization of art. No longer is the creation of stunning visuals reserved for highly trained illustrators and designers—now, anyone with an internet connection and a vivid imagination can produce compelling, original artwork. By leveraging advanced machine learning algorithms, Midjourney transforms textual prompts into vivid, often breathtaking images. Understanding how to guide this process effectively through careful prompt engineering unlocks a vast new realm of creativity.

One of Midjourney's standout features is its simplicity and accessibility. Unlike some AI art platforms that require standalone applications or significant hardware resources, Midjourney functions entirely within the Discord platform. Getting started is as easy as joining the official Midjourney server, typing a simple command, and beginning your creative journey. There are dedicated channels for newcomers, offering a welcoming space to experiment without crowding more advanced users.

At the heart of the platform is its text-to-image generation tool. By typing /imagine followed by your prompt, you initiate the creation process. The richness and specificity of your prompt determine the quality of the resulting image. For example, a basic prompt like "a cat" will yield a generic feline, while a more refined prompt—such as "a fluffy Persian cat sitting on a windowsill at sunset, glowing with golden hour light, hyperrealistic style"—will generate an image with significantly more visual nuance and emotional depth.

Prompt engineering is the core creative skill for Midjourney users. It's the practice of shaping your descriptions to accurately express the aesthetic, composition, and emotion you're aiming for. Including stylistic references—like "photorealistic," "watercolor," "Art Deco," or "surreal"—guides the model's output toward a desired visual identity. Descriptive terms such as "sharp," "dreamy," "dramatic lighting," or "ultra detailed" further enhance the outcome. Specificity is key: the more vivid and concrete your words, the closer the AI gets to your intended vision.

Midjourney typically generates four images in response to a single prompt. From there, you can upscale your favorite using the "U" buttons, or request additional variations using the "V" buttons. This allows for rapid iteration, making it easy to refine your concept through trial and error. It's a dynamic process, full of creative surprises and small, satisfying breakthroughs.

The applications of Midjourney stretch far beyond casual use. Artists, designers, writers, educators, marketers, and game developers all find unique value in the platform. A graphic novelist might prototype characters or scenes in different visual styles. A game designer could use Midjourney for rapid concept art. A social media marketer might generate bespoke graphics for a product campaign. Educators are also finding ways to bring complex subjects to life through visuals that support their teaching. The speed and flexibility of Midjourney make it an ideal creative partner in these fast-paced fields.

Compared to other tools in the AI art space, Midjourney stands out for its painterly, expressive style. Its images often lean toward the surreal or stylistic, making it ideal for fantasy, sci-fi, or conceptual projects. In contrast:

- **DALL·E 2**, developed by OpenAI, tends to offer more photorealistic images and supports *inpainting* (editing specific parts of an image), which Midjourney does not currently allow.

- **Stable Diffusion** is an open-source tool, prized for its flexibility and customizability. Artists can fine-tune models or even train their own styles, though it requires more technical setup.

- **Adobe Firefly** integrates seamlessly with Creative Cloud apps and is trained on licensed Adobe Stock images, making it a safer choice for commercial use within corporate environments.

While all of these tools offer powerful creative capabilities, Midjourney's strength lies in its balance of ease, community support, and artistic flair.

As you build confidence, you can explore more advanced techniques such as aspect ratio adjustments (e.g., --ar 3:2 for landscape formats), which allow you to tailor images for specific platforms like websites, posters, or social media. You can also use **negative prompts** to instruct Midjourney what *not* to include. For instance, a prompt for "a futuristic city skyline, --no dark, --no cluttered" can help filter out unwanted stylistic elements.

Another creative strategy is referencing artists or styles. Including "in the style of Van Gogh" or "inspired by Art

Nouveau" can guide the visual tone, though users should take care not to misappropriate or copy the work of living artists or culturally sensitive material.

Midjourney isn't just for solo projects. It also fosters creative collaboration. Multiple users in a team can generate ideas together, review visual directions in real time, and iterate rapidly on a shared vision. This streamlines concept development for design studios, game developers, and other creative teams.

As with all AI-powered tools, it's important to understand the boundaries. Midjourney is not flawless. It sometimes struggles with anatomy, perspective, or text rendering. Results can vary depending on how the model interprets a phrase. It's also essential to consider the broader ethical and legal implications of AI-generated art.

On ownership and commercial rights: As of now, users with a paid subscription to Midjourney are granted commercial usage rights for the images they generate. However, **copyright ownership of AI-generated images is not legally guaranteed in most jurisdictions**, as current laws typically require a human author for copyright to be assigned. This is an evolving area of law and worth monitoring for those planning to publish or sell AI-generated artwork.

In conclusion, Midjourney offers a groundbreaking new way to create visual art. It places a powerful tool in the hands of anyone willing to explore it. With a combination of thoughtful prompt engineering, creative experimentation, and ethical mindfulness, users can unlock astonishing new forms of expression. Whether you're prototyping a new graphic novel, designing campaign visuals, or simply creating art for the joy of it, Midjourney is an invitation to imagine—and see—what's possible when human creativity meets machine intelligence.

OTHER AI TOOLS: EXPLORING A RANGE OF APPLICATIONS

Beyond the captivating world of AI image generation, a vast and rapidly expanding ecosystem of AI tools is reshaping how we work, create, and interact with information. These technologies are streamlining workflows, boosting productivity, and unlocking new possibilities across countless industries. From enhancing our writing and simplifying coding to uncovering insights from complex data, AI is becoming an indispensable asset in both professional and personal spheres.

One of the most accessible and widely used categories of AI tools is writing assistance. Platforms like **Grammarly** and **ProWritingAid** go far beyond basic grammar and spell checks. These AI-powered services analyze tone, clarity, engagement, and consistency in your writing. Grammarly, for instance, can detect overuse of passive voice, suggest stronger vocabulary, and recommend stylistic adjustments tailored to your intended audience. ProWritingAid adds even more depth with features like sentence variety analysis, readability scores, and cliche detection. For writers, students, marketers, and anyone who communicates professionally, these tools provide real-time guidance to help polish and elevate written content. Many also include built-in **plagiarism detection**, reinforcing originality and academic integrity.

In software development, **AI-assisted coding** is revolutionizing how programmers approach their work. Tools like **GitHub Copilot**, powered by OpenAI, and **Tabnine**, built on open-source language models, offer intelligent code suggestions based on the context of what you're typing. These tools predict entire lines or blocks of code, reducing time spent on repetitive patterns and helping developers avoid syntax errors. For example, if you're writing a function to clean a dataset in Python, Copilot might anticipate the next few steps and offer a complete, well-structured snippet. While these assistants don't replace traditional coding skills, they function like a supportive pair programmer, boosting efficiency and helping developers focus on architecture and logic rather than boilerplate.

AI is also transforming the way we work with **data and analytics**. Tools like **Tableau** and **Microsoft Power BI** have integrated AI-driven features that assist in trend detection, anomaly spotting, and even automated data storytelling. Tableau's "Ask Data" feature allows users to ask plain-English questions of their data, while Power BI incorporates predictive analytics and machine learning models directly into dashboards. These enhancements reduce reliance on data science teams and make powerful insights accessible to business leaders, researchers, and educators. With AI doing the heavy lifting on the backend, users can spend more time making strategic decisions and less time wrangling spreadsheets.

The breadth of AI applications doesn't stop there. AI-driven **translation tools** like **DeepL** and **Google Translate** are facilitating seamless multilingual communication. Tools like **Otter.ai** and **Descript** offer accurate, real-time **transcription** and **podcast editing**, often with speaker identification and the ability to edit audio by editing the text transcript. **Summarization tools** like **SMMRY**, **QuillBot**, or even ChatGPT itself are helping users digest lengthy documents in seconds.

Meanwhile, **AI voice assistants** such as **Alexa**, **Google Assistant**, and **Siri** are becoming increasingly adept at handling nuanced commands, controlling smart devices, and offering reminders and recommendations customized to individual preferences.

In **healthcare**, AI tools are being developed to assist with early diagnosis, drug discovery, and personalized medicine. **IBM Watson Health** has been used to support clinical decision-making, while startups are developing tools that analyze imaging data to identify conditions like cancer or retinal disease earlier and more accurately. In **finance**, AI supports fraud detection, algorithmic trading, and customer service, streamlining operations while enhancing security and personalization.

As we embrace these tools, it's critical to remain mindful of the **ethical considerations** that accompany them. Concerns around algorithmic bias, data privacy, and job displacement are real and warrant proactive attention. Transparency in how algorithms operate and how data is used is essential to building public trust. Developing **clear regulatory frameworks**, ensuring **human oversight**, and implementing **ethical design standards** are all vital steps toward ensuring that AI development serves the public good rather than exacerbating existing inequalities.

AI's rapid evolution also means staying up-to-date is a moving target. New platforms and updates emerge constantly. Staying informed—whether through industry newsletters, webinars, online communities, or hands-on experimentation—is crucial to leveraging AI effectively. Lifelong learning isn't just a buzzword; it's a necessary mindset in a world where capabilities shift by the quarter, not the decade.

Gaining a **basic understanding of how AI works**—even if you're not a technologist—can significantly enhance how you use these tools. Concepts like **machine learning**, **natural language processing**, and **computer vision** underpin many of today's most powerful applications. A working knowledge of these ideas helps users better interpret results, avoid misuse, and choose the most appropriate tool for the task at hand.

The integration of AI into our daily lives is no longer a vision of the future; it's already here. From everyday conveniences like grammar checkers to highly specialized tools in medicine, law, design, and finance, AI is expanding what individuals and teams can accomplish. Used responsibly and with intention, these tools can elevate productivity, creativity, and quality of life. The challenge lies not just in adopting the latest AI tools, but in using them wisely, balancing innovation with ethics, and automation with human judgment.

AI is not replacing us, it's extending us. The future of AI depends on how we use it, what values we embed in its design, and how broadly we ensure access to its benefits. With awareness, curiosity, and responsibility, we can ensure that this expanding toolkit continues to serve humanity in meaningful and lasting ways.

TIPS AND TRICKS: MAXIMIZING THE EFFICIENCY OF AI TOOLS

Harnessing the full potential of AI tools isn't just about knowing what they can do—it's about knowing how to use them effectively. This involves understanding how to interact with these systems, fine-tuning their settings, and troubleshooting when things go awry. Think of it as learning the language of AI—a language that allows you to articulate your needs clearly and receive the best possible results. This chapter focuses on practical strategies to maximize the efficiency of AI tools, turning you from a casual user into a confident, skilled operator.

One of the most important techniques in working with AI, particularly natural language models like ChatGPT or Bard, is **prompt engineering**. A well-crafted prompt is the key to unlocking more accurate, useful, and creative responses. Instead of a general request like "Write a story," consider how much more specific and effective a prompt like this can be: "Write a short story about a robot learning to love, told in a whimsical tone with steampunk elements." That extra context gives the AI clearer direction, often producing more satisfying and relevant results.

The same principle applies to AI image generators such as Midjourney or DALL·E 2. Vague prompts like "a cat" might yield generic images, while a more descriptive version—"a photorealistic portrait of a fluffy Persian cat sitting in a sunbeam, painted in the style of Rembrandt"—provides much more context, leading to better visual outcomes. The more detail you provide, the closer the results will align with your vision.

Beyond prompt clarity, it's essential to understand the **parameters** available within each tool. Many platforms allow users to adjust settings that control things like creativity, length, tone, resolution, or aspect ratio. Experimenting with these options can significantly improve results. For example, if you're generating marketing copy, a higher creativity setting might yield fresh and engaging ideas. On the other hand, for technical documentation, dialing that setting down can produce clearer, more factual language. Similarly, in image generation tools, choosing the correct aspect ratio or lighting style can enhance the usability of your images for specific formats, whether it's a social media post or a printed flyer.

Another critical skill is **troubleshooting**. AI tools are powerful, but they aren't infallible. You may encounter issues like inaccurate outputs, awkward phrasing, or images that don't match your expectations. When this happens, take a systematic approach. First, review your prompt for clarity and specificity. Are you using the right keywords? Have you included enough detail? Next, check your settings—are they aligned with your goal? If you're still stuck, consult the tool's help documentation or online user forums. Most AI platforms have active communities that can provide guidance and share best practices.

Choosing the right tool for the job is another important consideration. Not every AI tool is designed to do everything.

For example, using a chatbot to analyze complex spreadsheets isn't likely to produce the best results—there are better-suited platforms for that, such as Power BI or Tableau. Similarly, while ChatGPT can generate basic code, developers may benefit more from tools like GitHub Copilot, which are specifically built for software development. Matching the task to the right tool saves time and avoids unnecessary frustration.

To stay efficient and informed, it's worth **keeping up with the latest developments** in the AI space. The field evolves quickly. New features, tools, and integrations are released frequently. Subscribing to newsletters, following AI thought leaders, attending webinars, and exploring product updates can help you stay ahead of the curve. Platforms change rapidly, and staying current can mean the difference between struggling with outdated methods and tapping into new capabilities that simplify your work.

A lesser-discussed but equally valuable technique is **breaking tasks into smaller steps**. Instead of feeding the AI a long, complicated instruction, try simplifying your task into a sequence of shorter, clearer requests. For example, rather than asking ChatGPT to write an entire business proposal in one go, ask it to outline the proposal first, then expand each section separately. This step-by-step method helps maintain coherence and allows you to guide the results as you go.

Finally, the most important mindset to adopt when using AI tools is **collaboration**. AI is not a replacement for your creativity or expertise, it's a partner. Interacting with AI should feel iterative and collaborative. YOU prompt. It responds. YOU revise. It adjusts. The more you engage, the better you'll understand how to coax out the best performance from your tools. Each session builds your intuition, teaching you what works, what doesn't, and how to shape better prompts or tweak outputs for improved results.

Mastering AI tools isn't a one-time milestone. It's an ongoing process of learning, adapting, and refining. By approaching this technology with curiosity, patience, and intention, you can unlock new levels of productivity, creativity, and problem-solving ability. The future of work is increasingly shaped by these tools, and those who learn to use them well will be best positioned to thrive in this evolving landscape.

Stay curious. Experiment often. And don't be afraid to iterate your way to excellence.

AI-POWERED DIAGNOSTICS: IMPROVING ACCURACY AND SPEED

The transformative potential of AI extends far beyond productivity tools and creative applications—it is reshaping healthcare itself, particularly in the realm of diagnostics. AI-powered diagnostic tools are dramatically improving the accuracy, speed, and efficiency of medical assessments, leading to earlier interventions and better patient outcomes. This is no longer theoretical. It is already happening, with measurable results.

One of the most impactful applications of AI in diagnostics is in **radiology**. Radiologists, often managing high volumes of complex imaging—X-rays, CT scans, MRIs—can now rely on AI as a powerful assistant. Trained on extensive datasets, AI algorithms can automatically detect anomalies, highlight potential areas of concern, and even offer preliminary diagnostic suggestions. Rather than replacing radiologists, these systems act as a second set of eyes, identifying details that might be missed in a high-pressure environment.

For instance, an AI tool might detect a tiny lung nodule in a chest X-ray—an early indicator of lung cancer—that a human reader could easily overlook during a busy shift. In emergency rooms and high-volume hospitals, AI can also prioritize critical cases, ensuring that life-threatening conditions receive immediate attention. The integration of AI in radiology is already yielding faster turnaround times, higher diagnostic accuracy, and better resource allocation.

In **pathology**, AI is also making a profound impact. Diagnosing diseases like cancer often depends on microscopic examination of tissue samples, a meticulous and sometimes subjective process. AI-powered systems can analyze digital slides with exceptional speed and precision, identifying abnormal cell structures, quantifying the presence of disease markers, and supporting pathologists with real-time insights. For example, AI tools have been shown to match or exceed human-level performance in identifying prostate and breast cancer cells in biopsy slides. This not only improves diagnostic reliability but also reduces the time needed to deliver results—an essential factor in patient outcomes.

AI's reach continues across other specialties:

- In **cardiology**, algorithms are being used to interpret ECGs and detect conditions like atrial fibrillation or left ventricular hypertrophy with high accuracy, sometimes outperforming generalist physicians.

- In **ophthalmology**, AI tools can analyze retinal images to identify early signs of diabetic retinopathy, glaucoma, and macular degeneration —diseases where early detection is critical to preventing vision loss.

- In **dermatology**, AI systems can evaluate skin

lesions, helping differentiate between benign moles and malignant melanomas, often with diagnostic accuracy on par with trained dermatologists.

Beyond clinical accuracy, AI has the potential to **expand access to care**, particularly in underserved or rural regions where specialists are in short supply. A general practitioner in a remote clinic, equipped with an AI tool, can analyze a patient's ECG or skin lesion and receive expert-level diagnostic support —instantly and affordably. AI also enables scalable screening programs, helping healthcare systems screen more patients more efficiently, especially in regions facing medical staff shortages.

However, realizing this promise depends on addressing several key **challenges and responsibilities.**

One is **bias**. AI systems are only as good as the data they are trained on. If those datasets lack representation from certain populations—such as people of color, women, or those from underserved regions—the algorithms may be less accurate for those groups. This is not a theoretical concern: studies have demonstrated racial disparities in AI performance in both dermatology and radiology. To build truly equitable diagnostic tools, datasets must reflect the diversity of the global population. Developers, researchers, and regulatory agencies must work collaboratively to test and improve algorithms across all demographic groups.

Another essential issue is **regulatory oversight**. Any diagnostic tool—especially those that influence patient treatment—must meet stringent standards for safety and efficacy. AI systems must be rigorously validated through clinical trials and subjected to review by national regulatory bodies such as the FDA in the United States or the EMA in Europe. Transparent evaluation processes and clear guidelines for approval are vital for earning the trust of clinicians and patients alike. Emerging efforts, like the FDA's proposed framework for AI-based software as a medical device (SaMD), are beginning to provide structure for this growing field.

Equally critical is **data privacy**. AI systems depend on vast amounts of medical data—images, lab results, personal health records. Protecting this data is non-negotiable. Healthcare providers and technology developers must comply with legal frameworks such as HIPAA (in the U.S.) and GDPR (in the EU), ensuring that patient information is encrypted, anonymized, and stored securely. Consent, transparency, and limited data access must be built into every layer of AI system design.

Despite these challenges, the **benefits of AI in diagnostics are undeniable**. It's not about replacing human clinicians but enhancing their capabilities. AI can help reduce human error, manage growing workloads, and provide clinical decision support, allowing healthcare professionals to spend more time with patients and less time on repetitive tasks.

Ultimately, the success of AI in healthcare will depend not just on technical innovation, but on **collaboration**: between data scientists and doctors, between regulators and developers, and between healthcare systems and patients. If we get this right, AI will not only improve diagnostic accuracy—it will help build a more accessible, equitable, and efficient healthcare system for all.

This is not just a story of machines becoming smarter. It's a story of how, with the right safeguards and shared goals, technology can help us care for one another more effectively and compassionately.

PERSONALIZED MEDICINE: TAILORING TREATMENTS TO INDIVIDUAL NEEDS

Personalized medicine represents a paradigm shift in healthcare —one that moves beyond the traditional "one-size-fits-all" model to deliver treatments tailored to the unique characteristics of each patient. Fueled by breakthroughs in genomics, proteomics, metabolomics, and other "omics" disciplines, this approach leverages massive volumes of biological data to inform clinical decisions. The complexity of this data, however, far exceeds the capacity of human clinicians to analyze alone. This is where artificial intelligence (AI) proves transformative unlocking insights, accelerating discovery, and refining patient care at an unprecedented scale.

AI's role in personalized medicine begins at the earliest stages: **drug discovery and development**. Historically, developing a new drug has been a time-consuming, costly, and high-risk process. AI dramatically enhances this process by rapidly analyzing databases of molecular structures, biological targets, and clinical data to identify promising drug candidates. Machine learning models can predict how compounds will interact with biological systems, flag potential toxicities, and estimate the likelihood of success in clinical trials. This enables researchers to focus on the most viable options, significantly reducing development timelines and R&D costs. For instance, companies like Atomwise and BenevolentAI use AI to repurpose existing drugs or identify new compounds with promising therapeutic profiles.

Beyond discovery, AI is transforming the way **clinical trials** are designed and conducted. Traditionally, trials rely on large, often heterogeneous patient cohorts. This can obscure meaningful results due to individual variation in response. AI helps researchers stratify patients into more homogenous subgroups based on genetic profiles, biomarkers, comorbidities, and lifestyle data. This targeted approach—known as precision enrollment—can lead to more efficient trials and more accurate efficacy assessments. Moreover, predictive algorithms can identify which patients are most likely to benefit from a treatment or experience adverse effects, further refining trial design and ethical integrity.

In oncology, this stratified approach is already being applied. AI algorithms analyze tumor sequencing data to match patients with therapies most likely to target their specific cancer mutations. In doing so, oncologists can avoid ineffective treatments and reduce exposure to unnecessary side effects, improving both survival rates and quality of life.

Once treatment begins, AI continues to deliver value by **monitoring patient responses in real-time**. Through electronic health records, wearable sensors, and imaging tools, AI systems gather ongoing data about a patient's health. These systems can detect patterns that indicate whether a treatment is working, whether side effects are emerging, or whether adjustments are needed. For example, AI tools can identify early signs of neutropenia in chemotherapy patients, enabling timely interventions that prevent complications. In chronic conditions like diabetes or hypertension, AI can assist in titrating medications based on a patient's continuous monitoring data, helping to maintain optimal control.

AI is also advancing **personalized diagnostics**. By analyzing complex datasets—genetic sequences, proteomic profiles, medical imaging, and clinical histories—AI tools can detect disease risk factors or early signs of illness. A good example is the use of AI in breast cancer screening, where algorithms analyze mammograms for subtle changes that may not be noticeable to the human eye, helping identify malignancies earlier. In cardiovascular medicine, AI is used to predict the likelihood of heart attacks by analyzing imaging, EKGs, and biomarkers. The earlier a disease can be identified and characterized, the more personalized and effective the intervention.

Yet, despite these powerful capabilities, integrating AI into personalized medicine comes with **several key challenges**.

First is the issue of **data quality and interoperability**. AI relies on large, diverse, and well-labeled datasets to learn effectively. However, data from different hospitals or systems often exist in incompatible formats, use different terminologies, or suffer from missing values. Efforts to standardize data collection and terminology—such as HL7's FHIR standards—are essential to building interoperable AI systems.

Second is the need for **interpretability**. Many of the most accurate AI models, such as deep neural networks, function as "black boxes," making decisions that are difficult for clinicians to understand or explain. In medicine, where decisions affect lives, transparency matters. Clinicians must be able to trust and interpret AI-driven recommendations. Developing explainable AI (XAI) systems is therefore a growing priority, enabling healthcare professionals to understand not just *what* the model predicts, but *why*.

Third, **data privacy and security** are non-negotiable. AI systems often rely on sensitive health information, raising concerns about how that data is stored, shared, and used. Ensuring compliance with frameworks like HIPAA and GDPR is essential. Robust encryption, anonymization techniques, and transparent data governance policies must be in place to protect patients and preserve trust.

Finally, the **economic barrier** cannot be ignored. Implementing AI solutions requires investment in computing infrastructure, software integration, staff training, and ongoing maintenance. For many hospitals and clinics, especially in low-resource settings, these costs can be prohibitive. Expanding access will depend on scalable, cost-effective AI solutions and collaborative models involving public-private partnerships and government support.

Despite these hurdles, the **promise of personalized medicine powered by AI is immense**. By aligning treatment with the unique biology, preferences, and conditions of each patient, this approach can:

- Increase treatment efficacy
- Reduce side effects and complications
- Improve overall patient satisfaction and outcomes
- Streamline care delivery and reduce unnecessary interventions

Moreover, as AI models continue to evolve and data becomes more accessible and standardized, the accuracy and personalization of care will only improve.

In conclusion, personalized medicine is not just a vision for the future, it is becoming a reality, driven by the growing capabilities of AI. While the road ahead requires careful attention to ethical, regulatory, and logistical issues, the destination holds transformative potential. With ongoing research, equitable implementation strategies, and a commitment to responsible innovation, AI-powered personalized medicine can help usher in an era of healthcare that is more precise, proactive, and patient-centered.

AI-ASSISTED SURGERY: ENHANCING PRECISION AND MINIMIZING RISKS

The integration of artificial intelligence (AI) into the operating room marks a transformative advancement in modern medicine. Far from replacing surgeons, AI-assisted surgery empowers them with tools that enhance precision, reduce invasiveness, and improve patient outcomes. This collaboration between surgical expertise and intelligent technology is redefining what's possible in the field of surgery and doing so safely, effectively, and with the patient's best interests at heart.

One of the most impactful contributions of AI in surgery lies in **medical image analysis**. Surgeons rely heavily on CT scans, MRIs, and ultrasound imaging to plan procedures and navigate complex anatomy. However, manually interpreting these images is time-consuming and leaves room for human error. Deep learning algorithms, trained on large datasets of annotated medical images, can now analyze scans with remarkable accuracy and speed. These tools can detect anomalies such as tumors, lesions, or internal bleeding that might otherwise go unnoticed, while also quantifying their size, location, and progression. This data-driven clarity helps surgeons plan more targeted and efficient procedures, reducing unnecessary incisions, minimizing tissue damage, and shortening recovery time.

AI's contributions go beyond preoperative planning. **During surgery**, AI-enhanced robotic systems are elevating the precision and safety of real-time operations. Systems like those developed by Intuitive Surgical (e.g., the da Vinci Surgical System) are being augmented with AI modules that offer real-time assistance. These systems provide haptic feedback, enhanced 3D visualization, and the ability to perform micro-adjustments with sub-millimeter accuracy. AI algorithms continuously track the positions of surgical tools in relation to delicate anatomical structures, offering visual cues and alerts to help surgeons avoid nerves, vessels, or organs, an essential function during high-risk procedures.

Additionally, AI is being used to support **intraoperative decision-making**. For example, in laparoscopic surgery where the surgeon's field of view is limited, AI systems can overlay critical information onto the video feed, such as highlighting anatomical landmarks, identifying surgical planes, or even suggesting step-by-step guidance based on the specific case and real-time data. By accessing extensive surgical databases and combining them with patient-specific data, AI can act like an expert assistant, quietly improving judgment and efficiency when it matters most.

Beyond robotics, AI enhances **image-guided surgeries**—procedures where surgeons use imaging to guide tools like catheters or needles. AI algorithms improve the accuracy of image registration (aligning imaging data with physical anatomy), leading to more precise placement of instruments. This increased accuracy has major implications for minimally invasive procedures, reducing risks, improving outcomes, and often eliminating the need for repeat interventions.

One particularly exciting application of AI is in **surgical training and simulation**. Mastering complex surgical skills takes years, and real-life training opportunities can be limited. AI-powered simulators are filling this gap. These advanced platforms create realistic, risk-free environments for practice, often paired with real-time feedback. AI can analyze a surgeon's technique, assess precision, speed, and decision-making, and offer constructive insights—enabling continuous improvement without putting patients at risk. This not only accelerates skill development but also supports ongoing professional development throughout a surgeon's career.

However, the rise of AI in surgery presents important **ethical and practical challenges**.

A primary concern is **accountability**. Even as AI assists with critical decisions, the surgeon remains ultimately responsible for the patient's outcome. It's essential that AI be treated as a support system—not a decision-maker—and that clear standards of liability are established. This includes creating strong regulatory frameworks to guide development and deployment, particularly in high-stakes environments like the operating room.

Another pressing issue is **transparency**. Many AI systems, especially those based on deep learning, operate as so-called "black boxes," offering little explanation for how they reach their conclusions. In surgery, where decisions must be backed by a clear rationale, this opacity poses a barrier to trust and adoption. The development of **explainable AI (XAI)**—models that offer insights into their reasoning—is essential for surgeons to feel confident integrating AI into their decision-making process.

Data privacy and security are also of paramount importance.

Training effective AI systems requires access to vast quantities of patient data—scans, records, operative notes—raising concerns about how this data is handled. Healthcare institutions must enforce robust governance policies, including strict access controls, anonymization protocols, and compliance with privacy laws like HIPAA in the United States and GDPR in Europe.

There are also **infrastructure and access challenges**. Running sophisticated AI systems requires high-performance computing capabilities, integration with hospital networks, and consistent software updates. These needs translate to significant financial costs, which can create disparities between well-funded urban hospitals and under-resourced clinics or rural facilities. Bridging this gap will require a combination of policy incentives, shared infrastructure models, and public-private collaborations to make AI-assisted surgery accessible and equitable.

Despite these hurdles, the **benefits of AI-assisted surgery are compelling and increasingly evident**. Enhanced precision, reduced complications, shorter recovery times, and expanded access to expert-level care are already being realized in operating rooms around the world. The future of surgery is not about replacing surgeons with machines, it's about augmenting their skills, insight, and decision-making capabilities with intelligent tools that elevate the standard of care.

As research and development continue, we can expect even more advanced applications: systems that learn from each procedure to refine future ones, collaborative platforms that support remote surgery or tele-mentoring, and personalized surgical approaches informed by the patient's unique anatomy and health profile.

In conclusion, AI-assisted surgery exemplifies the most promising form of technological innovation—one that amplifies human skill, promotes safety, and places the patient at the center. As this field continues to mature, it will be the partnership between human judgment and artificial intelligence that defines the next era of surgical excellence. This isn't just the future of surgery, it's already shaping the present, one carefully guided incision at a time.

AI IN PUBLIC HEALTH: PREVENTING AND MANAGING OUTBREAKS

The transformative power of artificial intelligence (AI) reaches far beyond individual care—it extends to the broader landscape of public health, where it is already reshaping how we anticipate, prevent, and manage outbreaks of infectious diseases. In a world where health threats can emerge and escalate rapidly, AI offers a crucial advantage: the ability to analyze massive, complex datasets and extract meaningful insights in real time. This makes AI a vital partner in enhancing global health security and emergency response systems.

One of the most promising applications of AI in public health is **predictive modeling**. By analyzing historical outbreaks, environmental factors, travel trends, and population demographics, AI algorithms can forecast where and when a disease may emerge or resurge. These models are data-rich and dynamic, incorporating variables like temperature, rainfall, humidity, vaccination coverage, and even social media posts that mention flu-like symptoms. This approach allows health officials to act early—mobilizing resources, distributing vaccines, and tailoring public messaging—before a crisis takes hold.

For instance, AI has already demonstrated its capabilities in forecasting **seasonal influenza** by analyzing data from emergency departments, weather trends, search engine queries, and social media. Similar techniques have been used to predict and monitor outbreaks of **dengue fever**, **Zika virus**, and **antibiotic-resistant infections**. By accurately predicting where these threats may occur, public health agencies are better equipped to respond proactively, saving lives and reducing the overall impact on health systems.

AI also plays a vital role in **real-time monitoring and outbreak management**. During an epidemic, the sheer volume of data generated, ranging from hospital records and lab tests to geolocation and social media data, can quickly overwhelm traditional systems. AI-driven platforms can process this information rapidly, highlighting emerging hotspots, identifying clusters of cases, and tracking the effectiveness of public health interventions. These insights support faster, more adaptive decision-making during crises, enabling health officials to shift strategies as needed.

A particularly impactful application is in **automated contact tracing**. Traditional contact tracing is labor-intensive, relying on interviews and manual follow-ups. AI-enhanced tools can analyze data from mobile phones, transportation networks, and payment systems to identify who may have come into contact with an infected individual, drastically reducing response time. However, these capabilities raise important **privacy and data ethics concerns**. Robust governance frameworks, transparent consent processes, and strict data security protocols must be in place to protect individual rights while allowing for the responsible use of these technologies.

In the clinical setting, AI is also improving the **speed and**

accuracy of diagnoses, which is critical during outbreaks of fast-spreading diseases. AI-powered image recognition systems can analyze chest X-rays, CT scans, or microscopic slides with high accuracy—helping clinicians quickly identify infections such as pneumonia, tuberculosis, or COVID-19. This accelerates treatment decisions and reduces diagnostic variability between providers and institutions, especially where experienced personnel may be limited.

Another important benefit of AI in public health is its role in **surveillance systems**. AI can detect subtle changes in health-related data, such as spikes in ER visits, pharmacy sales, or online search trends, that signal a potential outbreak. By flagging these anomalies early, public health officials can investigate and intervene before a situation escalates.

AI also contributes to **resource optimization** during outbreaks. Health emergencies often stretch resources thin, ventilators, hospital beds, personal protective equipment, and trained staff are all in limited supply. AI can help prioritize where and when to deploy these resources by analyzing real-time data, improving equity and efficiency in care delivery. This is especially critical in regions with limited infrastructure or vulnerable populations.

Perhaps one of the most groundbreaking contributions of AI lies in **vaccine and drug development**. AI platforms can sift through vast libraries of molecular data to identify potential drug targets, predict protein interactions, and simulate treatment responses. These tools dramatically accelerate the research process, allowing scientists to identify promising candidates and move them to clinical trials faster. During the COVID-19 pandemic, AI was instrumental in tracking viral mutations and guiding vaccine updates.

Despite these successes, the implementation of AI in public health is not without its **challenges**.

- **Data quality and bias**: AI models are only as good as the data they are trained on. If the underlying data reflects systemic inequities—such as limited testing in rural areas or underreporting among marginalized populations—the AI may inherit and even amplify those biases. This can lead to disparities in resource allocation or diagnostic accuracy.

- **Privacy and consent**: Many AI tools rely on sensitive personal data. Protecting this information requires robust encryption, compliance with privacy laws like HIPAA and GDPR, and user-friendly consent mechanisms that explain how data is used and why.

- **Transparency and trust**: Many AI models, particularly those based on deep learning, are difficult to interpret. For health officials to trust AI-generated insights, there needs to be a push for **explainable AI (XAI)**—systems that not only give answers but also show the reasoning behind them.

- **Global equity**: Not all countries or health systems have the infrastructure or expertise to deploy advanced AI tools. Bridging this digital divide will require international collaboration, funding support, and open-source AI solutions that are accessible to lower-income countries.

Looking forward, the success of AI in public health depends on **collaboration** between data scientists, healthcare professionals, public health officials, ethicists, and policymakers. A shared commitment to ethical design, transparency, and equitable access will ensure that these tools benefit everyone, not just those with the most resources.

In conclusion, AI is quickly becoming an indispensable ally in the fight against infectious diseases. Its ability to predict, detect, manage, and respond to outbreaks offers a blueprint for a more agile and resilient global health system. But with great power comes great responsibility. As we integrate AI into public health frameworks, we must do so thoughtfully, ethically, and inclusively, ensuring that its benefits extend to every corner of the globe.

The future of public health is being written in real time—with AI as both a co-author and a guide.

ETHICAL CONSIDERATIONS: DATA PRIVACY, ALGORITHMIC BIAS, AND ACCESS TO CARE

The integration of artificial intelligence into healthcare holds immense promise but it also presents profound ethical challenges. As AI systems become increasingly embedded in diagnostics, treatment, and patient monitoring, the urgency to address concerns around **data privacy**, **algorithmic bias**, and **equitable access** grows ever more critical. Failing to confront these issues risks deepening existing disparities, eroding public trust, and undermining the very goals AI aims to advance in medicine.

Protecting Patient Privacy in the Age of AI

At the heart of healthcare AI lies an insatiable appetite for data. From genetic profiles to lifestyle behaviors, AI systems require vast quantities of sensitive information to function effectively. But this reliance raises pressing questions about how that data is collected, stored, and shared.

Patient medical records are among the most sensitive forms of personal information. Improper use or exposure can lead to identity theft, insurance discrimination, or reputational harm. High-profile healthcare data breaches in recent years have only heightened these concerns.

To address these risks, developers and healthcare providers must implement **robust data protection protocols**, including end-to-end encryption, advanced anonymization techniques, and access controls that limit who can view and modify patient data. But technical safeguards alone are not enough.

Transparency is equally essential. Patients have the right to know what data is being collected, why it's being used, how it will be protected, and whether it will be shared with third parties. This means crafting **clear, accessible data use policies** —not buried in fine print—and enabling patients to exercise meaningful consent. Ethical use of data begins with treating patients not as data points, but as partners in their care.

Algorithmic Bias and Health Equity

AI models are shaped by the data they're trained on—and if that data reflects historical inequalities, so too will the models. This issue, known as **algorithmic bias**, poses a significant threat to fairness in healthcare.

For example, an AI system trained primarily on data from white, urban populations may perform poorly when applied to racially diverse or rural communities. The consequences can be severe: missed diagnoses, inappropriate treatment plans, or exclusion from life-saving interventions.

Bias can creep in from multiple sources:

- Underrepresentation of certain groups in the training data

- Socioeconomic disparities that skew data collection

> • Implicit biases of the engineers and institutions developing the systems

To counteract these risks, a **multilayered approach** is essential. First, datasets must be curated with diversity in mind—ensuring representation across race, gender, age, geography, and socioeconomic status. Second, algorithms must be rigorously validated on diverse test sets, not just in development labs. And third, models should be continuously monitored after deployment to catch and correct any unintended harms.

Ethical oversight bodies, comprising ethicists, clinicians, engineers, and community representatives, can help ensure that fairness is built into every stage of the AI lifecycle.

Bridging the Digital Divide

While AI has the potential to democratize access to healthcare, it also risks entrenching a **two-tiered system**: one where technologically advanced facilities reap the benefits, while others are left behind.

Many communities still lack the basic infrastructure broadband internet, updated hardware, or digital literacy training to effectively utilize AI-powered health tools. This digital divide compounds existing inequalities, especially in rural areas and low-income regions.

Ensuring equitable access to AI-driven care will require **deliberate, systemic action**:

- Public and private investment in digital infrastructure

- Subsidies and open-access models for AI tools

- Inclusive design principles that prioritize usability for non-experts

- Culturally sensitive outreach and education to build

trust in AI systems

Access must not be treated as a secondary concern or a downstream problem, it should be foundational to how these technologies are developed and deployed.

A Framework for Ethical AI in Healthcare

To guide the responsible integration of AI, healthcare systems must adopt an ethical framework grounded in the four foundational principles of biomedical ethics:

- **Autonomy**: Patients must have agency over their data and a clear understanding of how AI tools are used in their care.

- **Beneficence**: AI should aim to maximize positive outcomes and be deployed to genuinely improve health and well-being.

- **Non-maleficence**: Systems must be designed and monitored to minimize harm—whether from bias, misdiagnosis, or data misuse.

- **Justice**: Benefits must be distributed equitably, and access should not depend on geography, income, or education.

These principles should be embedded into every stage of AI development—from data sourcing to model training, from clinical testing to long-term evaluation.

Building a Culture of Ethical Responsibility

Ethics cannot be an afterthought. It must be integrated into **organizational culture and training**, so that developers, clinicians, and administrators alike understand the social and moral dimensions of AI. Educational programs and interdisciplinary collaboration—between AI experts, ethicists, legal scholars, and patient advocates—are vital.

Independent review boards should be established to evaluate the ethical impact of new AI technologies before and after they are introduced into clinical settings. These bodies must have the authority to pause or modify deployments when risks outweigh benefits.

Transparency and public accountability are key. Regular audits, open reporting of outcomes, and public engagement are critical for maintaining trust. As AI systems grow more powerful, so too must our mechanisms for ensuring they are used fairly and responsibly.

A Global Effort Toward Ethical AI

Many of these challenges are global in nature. Data privacy regulations, such as **GDPR** in Europe or **HIPAA** in the U.S., are essential frameworks—but more coordination is needed across borders to standardize ethical practices and promote international cooperation. Equitable access to AI technologies should not depend on a country's GDP.

Open-source models, public sector investment, and knowledge-sharing initiatives will be essential to avoid a future where healthcare AI benefits only the wealthiest nations and institutions.

In conclusion, the promise of AI in healthcare is immense—but so is the responsibility. Data privacy, bias, and access are not peripheral concerns; they are central to whether AI helps or harms. The path forward must be paved with transparency, inclusivity, and a firm commitment to ethical principles.

If AI is to reshape healthcare for the better, it must do so in the service of all people, not just the privileged few. That is the real measure of progress.

SELF-DRIVING CARS: TECHNOLOGY AND ITS IMPLICATIONS

The transition to a world with self-driving cars is more than a technological leap, it is a fundamental reimagining of how we move through our environments. To understand this shift, we must examine both the sophisticated technology driving these vehicles and the profound societal implications of their widespread adoption.

The Technology Behind Autonomy

At the core of autonomous vehicles lies a fusion of advanced hardware and intelligent software. This ecosystem begins with a robust **sensor suite**, functioning as the vehicle's sensory organs:

- **Lidar** (Light Detection and Ranging) emits laser pulses to construct detailed 3D maps of the vehicle's surroundings, measuring distance and object shape with high precision.

- **Radar** (Radio Detection and Ranging) uses radio waves to detect the speed and position of nearby objects, especially useful in poor visibility.

- **Cameras** provide rich visual context, helping identify lane markings, road signs, traffic signals, and pedestrians.

- **Ultrasonic sensors**, common in parking systems, detect objects in close proximity, assisting with low-speed maneuvers.

These systems generate an enormous volume of raw data, which must be processed in real-time. This is where **artificial intelligence** plays a central role.

AI: The Brain of the Vehicle

AI algorithms, primarily based on **deep learning**, interpret the sensor data and translate it into actionable decisions. **Convolutional neural networks** (CNNs) excel at analyzing visual inputs, such as recognizing pedestrians or reading traffic signs. **Recurrent neural networks** (RNNs), and other time-series models, help predict the behavior of moving objects, like another car's path at an intersection.

These systems not only interpret the present moment but also anticipate potential risks, enabling the vehicle to plan routes and react to hazards before they arise.

The **planning and control systems** then take over. Path planning algorithms determine the safest, most efficient route, while **motion planning** converts this into a sequence of physical actions—steering, braking, and acceleration—executed with sub-second precision. The control system interfaces directly with the vehicle's hardware, continuously adjusting its behavior in response to new data.

Real-World Challenges

Despite impressive progress, deploying fully autonomous vehicles in the real world is complex. Unlike controlled test environments, public roads are unpredictable. Human drivers, pedestrians, animals, changing weather, road construction, and poorly marked lanes all present challenges that demand nuanced and context-aware decision-making.

Achieving **Level 5 autonomy**—vehicles capable of handling all driving tasks in all conditions without human intervention—remains a significant hurdle. Current systems, such as those developed by Waymo and Tesla, operate mostly at **Level 2 to Level 4**, requiring varying levels of driver supervision or limited operational domains.

Ethical Dilemmas and Regulation

As autonomous vehicles make decisions once reserved for human judgment, **ethical questions** emerge. In rare but inevitable accident scenarios, how should the vehicle prioritize outcomes? Should it favor the safety of its passengers or that of pedestrians? These questions have sparked intense debate and highlight the need for transparent, consistent ethical frameworks.

At the same time, **legal and regulatory systems** must evolve to define liability. If a self-driving car causes a crash, who is responsible, the software developer, the automaker, or the passenger? These legal ambiguities must be resolved before widespread deployment is possible.

Societal and Economic Implications

The widespread adoption of autonomous vehicles could **dramatically improve road safety**, given that human error is responsible for over 90% of traffic accidents. Improved coordination between vehicles could reduce congestion and travel times, lower fuel consumption, and cut carbon emissions.

Self-driving cars could also **transform urban design**. With less need for parking near destinations, cities could repurpose valuable real estate for green spaces, housing, or public use. Autonomous vehicles could also **expand mobility access** for individuals with disabilities, the elderly, or those without a driver's license.

On the other hand, this transition poses risks. **Millions of jobs in transportation**, including truck, taxi, and delivery drivers, may be displaced. Proactive policies such as retraining programs, income support, and new job creation will be essential to ease this economic shift.

Another pressing issue is **cybersecurity**. With vehicles relying on software and constant connectivity, they are vulnerable to hacking, software bugs, or malicious attacks. Ensuring robust, secure architectures and rigorous testing protocols is vital to protect passengers and public infrastructure.

The Road Ahead

The regulatory landscape remains fragmented. Countries like the United States, Germany, China, and Japan are taking varied approaches to testing and deployment, often led by private industry initiatives. Establishing global **standards for safety, liability, data usage, and testing protocols** will be essential to ensure interoperability and public confidence.

In the meantime, companies such as **Waymo, Cruise, Tesla, Mobileye, and Aurora** continue to push the boundaries of autonomous technology, often in collaboration with automakers and public agencies.

Conclusion

The road to autonomy is long and complex, but the destination is a transformative one. If developed and deployed responsibly, self-driving cars could deliver profound benefits in safety, efficiency, accessibility, and sustainability. But these benefits can only be realized by addressing the technical, legal, ethical, and social challenges that stand in the way.

The transition demands more than engineering excellence. It requires thoughtful regulation, public trust, and cross-sector collaboration. The journey is ongoing, but the potential to reshape how we live, work, and move is within reach.

AUTONOMOUS TRUCKS AND LOGISTICS: REVOLUTIONIZING SUPPLY CHAINS

The revolution in autonomous vehicles extends far beyond passenger cars, it is poised to fundamentally reshape the landscape of freight transportation and logistics. Autonomous trucks, guided by sophisticated artificial intelligence (AI) systems, are emerging as transformative tools in streamlining supply chains. Their potential to increase efficiency, reduce costs, and enhance safety could have sweeping implications for the global economy and the way goods are moved across regions and continents.

The Efficiency Imperative

Among the most significant advantages of autonomous trucking is its potential to drastically improve operational efficiency. Human drivers require rest breaks, limited hours of service, and time off, all of which contribute to downtime and extended delivery timelines. In contrast, autonomous trucks can operate around the clock, provided adequate charging or refueling infrastructure is in place. This continuous operation translates directly into faster deliveries and improved on-time performance, crucial in today's just-in-time inventory models.

AI-driven route optimization adds another layer of efficiency. These algorithms dynamically adjust routes based on real-time data such as traffic conditions, weather patterns, road closures, and delivery schedules. This reduces idle time, minimizes fuel consumption, and enables tighter logistics scheduling, resulting in substantial cost savings.

Safety and Situational Awareness

Beyond efficiency, autonomous trucks offer the potential for significantly improved road safety. Human error is a leading cause of trucking accidents. AI-powered driving systems, on the other hand, are programmed to adhere strictly to traffic laws, remain alert 100% of the time, and react instantaneously to unexpected events.

These trucks are equipped with advanced sensor suites—lidar, radar, cameras, and ultrasonic sensors—that work in concert to perceive the vehicle's surroundings with a level of accuracy that often surpasses human capabilities. In low visibility or inclement weather, these sensors provide consistent situational awareness, improving hazard detection and collision avoidance.

Optimizing Freight and Load Planning

AI can also revolutionize load management. By analyzing massive datasets, covering delivery windows, cargo type, destination demand, and weather forecasts, AI can optimize delivery schedules, balance vehicle loads, and reduce empty miles. This minimizes wear and tear on vehicles, reduces greenhouse gas emissions, and ensures that shipments arrive at their destinations more reliably.

Furthermore, AI can assist with real-time decision-making during unexpected disruptions, such as route closures or equipment malfunctions, allowing logistics operators to reroute and reallocate assets with minimal delay.

Roadblocks to Implementation

However, the path to widespread deployment of autonomous trucks is not without obstacles. Regulatory frameworks remain fragmented and under development. These vehicles must be tested rigorously across a variety of geographies, weather conditions, and use cases to meet safety and performance standards. Developing consistent regulations across national and international jurisdictions requires collaboration between government agencies, manufacturers, and the freight industry.

Public trust also remains a barrier. Concerns about safety, job displacement, and system reliability must be addressed through transparent communication, public education, and pilot programs that demonstrate the benefits of technology in real-world applications.

Economic and Labor Impacts

The trucking industry employs millions of people globally, many of whom rely on driving as their primary source of income. While autonomous technology will likely reduce the number of long-haul driving jobs, it will also create new roles in fleet management, remote vehicle monitoring, system maintenance, logistics coordination, and AI development.

To minimize economic disruption, proactive strategies must be put in place. These include vocational retraining programs, apprenticeships in new logistics technologies, and support for displaced workers to transition into adjacent industries.

Infrastructure and Cybersecurity

The rollout of autonomous trucking will require substantial upgrades to infrastructure. This includes investment in electric charging stations, 5G communication networks for real-time data exchange, and smart road infrastructure with clearer lane markings and signage. These investments will need to be supported by public-private partnerships and coordinated across regions.

Cybersecurity is another pressing concern. Autonomous trucks rely on highly interconnected software systems, making them potential targets for cyberattacks. Protecting these systems requires end-to-end encryption, intrusion detection systems, frequent software updates, and strict cybersecurity protocols. The consequences of a breach—whether it's a ransomware attack or a hacked navigation system—could be catastrophic to both public safety and supply chain continuity.

Environmental and Societal Benefits

Autonomous trucks offer potential environmental benefits by reducing fuel use through more efficient driving patterns and optimized logistics. When paired with electric drivetrains, they could dramatically reduce emissions, aligning the freight sector with global climate goals. Additionally, autonomous delivery capabilities could expand access to remote or underserved regions, improving economic inclusion and quality of life in rural communities.

The Road Ahead

The integration of AI into trucking is set to define the future of global logistics. Continued innovation will focus on increasing the reliability of autonomous systems under challenging road and weather conditions, improving human-AI collaboration for hybrid operations, and developing universal safety standards.

The successful rollout of autonomous freight systems will require ongoing collaboration between industry stakeholders, researchers, governments, and the public. By addressing regulatory, economic, and ethical concerns with foresight and coordination, we can unlock the enormous potential of AI-powered logistics.

The journey is complex, but the reward, a safer, faster, more sustainable global supply chain, is well worth the effort. As this transformation unfolds, it will not only reshape the trucking industry but redefine how we think about the movement of goods in the 21st century.

AI-POWERED TRAFFIC MANAGEMENT: OPTIMIZING FLOW AND REDUCING CONGESTION

The transformative power of artificial intelligence (AI) extends beyond autonomous vehicles—it is revolutionizing how we manage traffic itself. AI-powered traffic management systems are emerging as essential components of smart cities, offering a future where congestion is minimized, travel times are reduced, and transportation networks operate with unprecedented efficiency.

These systems leverage machine learning and advanced data analytics to process vast amounts of real-time information, predict traffic patterns, identify bottlenecks, and dynamically adjust signals to optimize the movement of vehicles across urban environments.

From Static Signals to Adaptive Intelligence

Imagine a city where traffic lights no longer follow rigid pre-programmed cycles but instead adapt intelligently to real-time conditions. This is the promise of AI-powered traffic systems. By analyzing data from traffic cameras, GPS-enabled vehicles, embedded roadway sensors, and even social media feeds, AI systems create a comprehensive, real-time map of traffic conditions.

For example, during peak hours, an AI-powered system might detect an increase in traffic volume at a major intersection. Instead of following a static cycle, it could dynamically extend green light durations in high-volume directions, reduce idle times, and balance flows to prevent backups. These adjustments can reduce fuel consumption, shorten commute times, and significantly enhance overall traffic flow.

Incident Detection and Rapid Response

AI also plays a pivotal role in incident detection and management. By continuously analyzing data from camera feeds and sensor networks, AI can quickly detect traffic anomalies such as accidents, stalled vehicles, or construction delays. This enables transportation authorities to reroute traffic, notify emergency services, and inform drivers through digital signage or navigation apps.

This proactive approach minimizes disruptions and reduces the likelihood of secondary accidents caused by sudden slowdowns or driver confusion.

Predictive Modeling and Infrastructure Planning

Beyond real-time management, AI excels in predicting traffic patterns by analyzing historical data, weather forecasts, public event calendars, and online search behavior. This predictive modeling enables cities to prepare for congestion before it happens, optimizing staffing, enforcement, and signal configurations in advance.

AI-driven models also inform long-term infrastructure planning. Urban designers can use insights from traffic simulations to determine where to add lanes, redesign intersections, or prioritize public transit investments. In some cases, AI has helped justify the development of intelligent parking systems that direct drivers to open spaces, reducing the time spent circling for parking—a major contributor to congestion.

Integration with Smart City Systems

AI-powered traffic management doesn't exist in a vacuum. When integrated with other smart city technologies, its impact multiplies. For instance, by coordinating with public transportation schedules, AI systems can give buses and trams signal priority, improving reliability and encouraging public transit use.

Environmental sensors can feed data into traffic models to reroute traffic away from areas with poor air quality. Similarly, smart parking platforms connected to traffic systems can guide vehicles more efficiently, further reducing congestion and emissions.

These interconnected technologies form the backbone of Intelligent Transportation Systems (ITS), which aim to make urban mobility safer, greener, and more efficient.

Implementation Challenges

Despite its promise, deploying AI-powered traffic systems comes with significant challenges.

1. Data Privacy and Security
AI systems often rely on sensitive location and behavioral data. Protecting user privacy requires strong encryption, data anonymization, and clear governance policies. Transparency about how data is collected and used is essential to maintaining public trust.

2. Standardization and Interoperability

Different agencies and vendors may use incompatible data formats, making integration difficult. Standardizing data formats and communication protocols is crucial for seamless operation across jurisdictions and platforms.

3. Computational Infrastructure
Processing real-time data from thousands of sensors and cameras demands substantial computing power. Cloud infrastructure may be required for scalability and resilience, especially for systems that must respond instantly to changes in traffic patterns.

4. Public Perception and Equity
There are concerns that advanced traffic systems may benefit some areas more than others, leading to unequal service quality. Cities must ensure that investments in AI-driven traffic systems are equitably distributed, benefiting underserved neighborhoods as much as affluent ones.

A Path Forward

Despite these hurdles, the benefits of AI-powered traffic management are clear. Reduced congestion, faster travel times, fewer emissions, and improved safety are all within reach. As cities continue to grow, the need for efficient, scalable transportation solutions becomes ever more urgent.

AI offers a path forward—not as a silver bullet, but as a powerful enabler of smarter, more responsive cities. With careful planning, ethical oversight, and public engagement, AI can play a central role in reimagining urban mobility for the 21st century.

AIR AND RAIL TRANSPORTATION: AI'S ROLE IN ENHANCING SAFETY AND EFFICIENCY

The revolution in autonomous vehicles is just one dimension of artificial intelligence's (AI) transformative impact on transportation. Equally significant—but less visible—are the advancements in AI within air and rail systems. These sectors, vital to national infrastructure and global commerce, are being quietly reshaped by AI technologies that promise enhanced safety, operational efficiency, and dramatically improved passenger experience.

AI in Air Traffic Control: From Prediction to Prevention

Air traffic control (ATC) is a domain overwhelmed by complexity. Each day, thousands of flights cross global airspace, requiring flawless coordination to prevent collisions and maintain efficient routing. While traditional ATC systems have served us remarkably well, increasing air traffic is pushing them to their limits.

AI offers a powerful solution. Algorithms trained on decades of historical flight data, weather patterns, and real-time positioning information can process immense datasets far more rapidly and accurately than humans. These systems help identify potential flight conflicts, optimize routing, and dynamically adjust schedules to minimize delays while enhancing safety.

One of the most promising applications is in **collision avoidance**. AI can analyze live flight paths, wind conditions, and other dynamic variables to forecast and prevent potential conflicts. These predictive models not only alert controllers and pilots early but also facilitate smoother navigation across crowded skies.

AI also supports **air traffic flow management**, using predictive modeling to detect bottlenecks before they occur. During high-traffic periods or adverse weather conditions, AI enables proactive rerouting and scheduling, reducing congestion and keeping flights on time.

In addition, AI can **automate routine air traffic management tasks** such as flight tracking, aircraft handoffs, and pilot communications. By handling repetitive duties, AI frees up human controllers to focus on complex, high-stakes decision-making, improving overall system performance. This collaboration between AI and human expertise ensures that safety and efficiency are not compromised.

The Need for Explainability and Security

Integrating AI into airspace operations brings challenges, particularly around transparency and reliability. In critical environments like ATC, controllers must trust AI recommendations and understand the reasoning behind them. This makes **explainable AI (XAI)** essential. Ensuring that systems offer not just accurate suggestions, but interpretable ones.

Equally important is **cybersecurity**. Any compromise in an AI-based ATC system could lead to catastrophic consequences. These platforms must be rigorously protected against breaches and manipulation, with strict protocols for redundancy and manual override when needed.

AI in Rail Transport: Predictive, Preventative, and Passenger-Focused

In rail transport, AI is improving both **infrastructure management** and **passenger services**. A standout application is **predictive maintenance**. AI systems continuously analyze real-time data from train sensors to monitor variables such as vibration, temperature, and pressure. By identifying anomalies early, rail operators can conduct preventative maintenance, avoiding breakdowns and service disruptions. This not only improves safety but also lowers maintenance costs and extends the lifespan of expensive rolling stock.

Another area of impact is **train scheduling**. AI algorithms can optimize train timetables by analyzing demand forecasts, track availability, and maintenance needs. Unlike traditional scheduling systems, AI-powered platforms can adapt in real-time—reallocating trains during peak hours, minimizing wait times, and even rerouting services to prevent delays. The result is a more responsive and efficient rail network.

Passenger experience is also being enhanced through **AI-powered customer service**. Chatbots and virtual assistants can provide real-time information on schedules, platform changes, and service disruptions. Meanwhile, smart recommendation systems offer travel alternatives during delays, or compensation suggestions where applicable. Real-time updates delivered via apps or station displays keep travelers informed and reduce frustration.

Implementation Challenges in Rail and Air

Deploying AI in these safety-critical sectors requires robust **data infrastructure, high-speed processing**, and **interoperable systems** across vendors and agencies. Ensuring **data privacy** and securing sensitive passenger or system data are non-negotiable. AI systems must comply with stringent cybersecurity standards, and fallback systems must be in place in case of failure.

Explainability is especially important in rail environments where decisions—such as rerouting trains or diagnosing a mechanical failure—must be transparent to maintenance teams and dispatchers. Trust in AI decisions is essential to safe and efficient adoption.

A Future of Seamless, Intelligent Mobility

Despite the technical and ethical hurdles, AI's integration into air and rail systems represents a critical step toward a more intelligent, sustainable transportation infrastructure. Enhanced safety, reduced delays, improved maintenance efficiency, and superior passenger experiences are all within reach.

The road ahead will require continued **collaboration among engineers, regulators, transportation authorities, and the public**. Investments in secure data platforms, training, and cross-sector standards are vital to scaling these innovations safely and equitably.

As AI systems become more sophisticated and reliable, they will not replace human oversight, but they will vastly extend their reach and precision. From crowded airports to sprawling rail networks, AI is quietly enabling a future where travel is not only more efficient but also safer, smarter, and more human-centered.

SAFETY AND REGULATION: ADDRESSING THE CHALLENGES OF AUTONOMOUS SYSTEMS

The transformative potential of autonomous transportation is undeniable, offering the promise of safer, more efficient, and more convenient mobility. Yet, the widespread adoption of these systems hinges on our ability to address critical safety and regulatory challenges. For autonomous systems to gain public trust and societal acceptance, they must be proven not only technologically sound but also subject to rigorous oversight and ethical standards. Meeting this challenge requires a comprehensive strategy involving robust safety protocols, forward-looking regulation, and transparent public engagement.

Safety as a Foundational Principle

Ensuring the safety of autonomous vehicles is among the most urgent priorities. Unlike human drivers, autonomous systems lack intuition and emotional judgment—traits that often play a role in navigating unpredictable real-world scenarios. Accidents involving autonomous vehicles, even when caused by surrounding human drivers, can erode public confidence and highlight system vulnerabilities.

To counter this, safety testing must extend beyond conventional crash simulations. Autonomous vehicles must be evaluated across a wide array of conditions, including inclement weather, complex urban intersections, rural environments, and scenarios involving erratic behavior from other drivers or pedestrians. These tests should include standardized simulation environments and real-world pilots, verified by independent third-party evaluators. Global harmonization of safety benchmarks will also be crucial to ensure consistency across jurisdictions and build international trust.

Equally important is ensuring redundancy within autonomous systems. Core components, such as perception modules, braking systems, and steering controls, must have fail-safes and backup functions. These redundancies should be independently verified to prevent cascading failures in the event of a system malfunction.

Infrastructure for Safe Integration

The success of autonomous systems is not determined solely by the vehicles themselves. Their safe integration depends on smart, responsive infrastructure. This includes high-definition maps for precise localization, reliable communication systems for vehicle-to-infrastructure (V2I) and vehicle-to-vehicle (V2V) communication, and embedded environmental sensors to monitor conditions in real-time.

Investment in smart infrastructure is critical. Inadequate GPS reception, outdated road markings, or the absence of V2I systems can compromise navigation and decision-making.

Without this supportive ecosystem, even the most advanced autonomous vehicles may perform unreliably or unsafely.

Regulatory Evolution and Legal Clarity

Most current traffic regulations assume a human driver behind the wheel. As a result, many existing laws are insufficient, or even incompatible, with the operation of autonomous systems. New legal frameworks must be developed to define key issues such as:

- **Liability in the event of an accident**
- **Data collection and privacy standards**
- **Cybersecurity requirements and audit procedures**
- **Certification processes for autonomous vehicle deployment**

These regulations should be internationally coordinated to avoid fragmented policies that hinder innovation or create regulatory loopholes. Clear, adaptable, and transparent legal structures are essential for both innovation and public protection.

Transparency and Public Engagement

Building public trust in autonomous transportation depends on openness and communication. Developers and regulators must clearly communicate the capabilities and limitations of these systems. That includes how decisions are made in edge cases, how personal data is used and protected, and how ethical dilemmas are approached.

Open data initiatives—where anonymized testing data is made available for public review—can increase accountability and allow researchers and journalists to independently assess safety and performance. Similarly, explainable AI (XAI) is critical. Users, regulators, and accident investigators must be able to understand how an autonomous system reached a decision, especially when safety is at stake.

Ethical Considerations and Social Input

One of the most difficult challenges in regulating autonomous systems is encoding ethics into machines. In unavoidable accident scenarios, vehicles may need to prioritize harm minimization. How these decisions are programmed, and who determines the value hierarchy involved, raises profound ethical questions.

Rather than leaving such decisions to developers alone, there should be multidisciplinary collaboration involving ethicists, policymakers, and public stakeholders. Societal values must be reflected in algorithm design, and public input should shape the ethical boundaries within which autonomous systems operate.

Cybersecurity and System Integrity

The software-intensive nature of autonomous systems makes them attractive targets for cyberattacks. A compromised vehicle could be manipulated remotely, posing serious risks to passengers and the public. Ensuring system integrity demands:

- Encrypted communication between vehicle systems
- Continuous vulnerability testing and software patching
- Redundant communication pathways and emergency shutdown protocols
- Mandatory cybersecurity compliance audits across supply chains

Cybersecurity isn't optional, it is foundational to public safety and confidence in autonomous mobility.

Economic Impact and Workforce Transition

Autonomous systems are likely to displace significant numbers of workers in transportation sectors, including trucking, ride-hailing, and delivery services. A proactive response is needed to manage this economic disruption. Policymakers must invest in reskilling and upskilling programs, support job transitions into adjacent industries (such as robotics maintenance or logistics management), and consider temporary income support for displaced workers.

At the same time, access to autonomous transportation must be equitable. Urban and rural communities alike should benefit from the efficiencies these technologies offer. This requires inclusive policies, subsidies for underserved areas, and efforts to ensure affordability.

A Path Forward

Autonomous transportation is no longer a future concept. It's an emerging reality. But its success depends on far more than technical performance. We must ensure safety, clarify regulations, address ethical complexity, and build systems that the public can trust.

Through collaborative planning, adaptive regulation, and transparent communication, we can shape a transportation future that is not only more intelligent, but also more just, resilient, and inclusive. The goal is not merely to build machines that drive themselves—but to design a system that serves people better than ever before.

ADAPTING TO CHANGE: DEVELOPING FUTURE-PROOF SKILLS

The previous sections explored AI's transformative influence and the importance of developing AI literacy. But understanding how AI is changing the world is only part of the equation. To truly thrive in this evolving landscape, we must actively adapt —cultivating skills that remain valuable and relevant in an AI-driven future. This isn't about fearing automation; it's about leveraging AI to enhance human creativity, productivity, and resilience. It's about becoming future-proof.

Adaptability: The Cornerstone of Future Readiness

In the age of rapid technological change, adaptability is essential. The skills valued today may be obsolete tomorrow. That's why **lifelong learning** is no longer optional, it's a prerequisite for career longevity and personal growth.

Embracing a **growth mindset**, the belief that abilities and intelligence can be developed through effort, fosters this adaptability. Seek out learning opportunities through online courses, workshops, books, or informal exploration. Curiosity and experimentation are powerful tools. Even failures become stepping stones when approached with a learner's mindset.

Critical Thinking in the Age of Algorithms

As AI becomes more integrated into our daily lives, **critical thinking** becomes increasingly important. While AI systems can process information quickly and at scale, they are not immune to error, bias, or flawed data.

Developing critical thinking means questioning assumptions, recognizing patterns of bias, and distinguishing fact from fiction. It's about understanding the limits of AI and knowing when human judgment is necessary. This discernment is essential in a world where misinformation spreads rapidly and technology's influence grows deeper.

Problem-Solving: A Human Superpower

While AI can automate many tasks, **complex problem-solving** remains uniquely human. The ability to identify problems, explore multiple solutions, and adapt ideas to changing circumstances is a skill that AI can support—but not replace.

Creative problem-solving involves both logic and imagination. It's about thinking laterally, trying new approaches, and learning from iteration. In an unpredictable world, this flexibility and inventiveness are increasingly valuable.

Creativity and Innovation: Partnering with AI

Some worry that AI will outpace human creativity—but the more likely future is one of **collaboration**, not competition. AI tools can inspire, assist, and augment creative processes in writing, design, music, and more.

Creativity and innovation are more than artistic skills— they're about generating new ideas, exploring possibilities, and challenging the status quo. As AI takes over routine tasks, creative thinking becomes one of the most sought-after human abilities.

Communication and Collaboration in a Digital World

In an AI-enhanced workplace, strong **communication and collaboration** skills are indispensable. Whether working across departments or cultures, the ability to clearly express ideas, actively listen, and build trust remains crucial.

Communicating about technology—especially its implications —requires clarity and empathy. It also means working well with interdisciplinary teams, often alongside AI systems or data-centric tools. Collaboration will increasingly involve human-to-AI and human-to-human interactions alike.

Complementary Technical Skills

While not everyone needs to become an AI developer, technical literacy can greatly improve your job prospects. Skills in **data science**, **cybersecurity**, **AI ethics**, and **human-AI interaction** will be in high demand.

Rather than compete with AI, aim to **complement** it. Learn how to interpret and visualize data, recognize algorithmic bias, or use no-code AI tools. These hybrid capabilities—technical fluency combined with domain expertise—will be a powerful differentiator.

Emotional Intelligence: The Human Advantage

As automation advances, **emotional intelligence (EQ)** remains a distinctly human strength. Understanding others' emotions, managing your own, and building empathetic relationships will be vital in healthcare, education, management, customer service, and beyond.

AI cannot replicate authentic empathy. **Compassion, active listening, and interpersonal sensitivity** are irreplaceable in fields where human connection matters most.

Digital and Data Literacy

Being comfortable with technology goes far beyond knowing how to use apps. **Digital literacy** involves understanding how digital tools affect privacy, behavior, communication, and society. It also includes awareness of how algorithms shape our online experience and what safeguards are necessary.

Similarly, **data literacy**—the ability to interpret, analyze, and act on data—is rapidly becoming a core workplace skill. As AI generates increasing volumes of information, those who can draw insights from data will have a strategic advantage.

Lifelong Learning and Career Adaptation

To future-proof your career, commit to **lifelong learning**. Stay current with emerging technologies. Use platforms like Coursera, LinkedIn Learning, edX, or Udemy to upskill regularly. Attend webinars, listen to industry podcasts, and follow thought leaders in your field.

Join professional communities, find mentors, and participate in events that keep you connected to industry shifts. Networking isn't just about finding your next opportunity—it's about keeping your thinking fresh and your mindset open to change.

Becoming a Co-Creator of the Future

Ultimately, developing future-proof skills is about taking ownership of your path in a world that is rapidly changing. It means moving from passive observer to **active participant**. It means shaping your relationship with AI not with fear, but with confidence and curiosity.

We are entering an era where the most valuable people won't be the ones who resist change, but those who adapt with agility, lead with empathy, and create value alongside intelligent machines.

The future is not something to be feared. It is something to be shaped—with your skills, your mindset, and your willingness to grow.

EMBRACING AI: HARNESSING ITS POWER FOR PERSONAL AND PROFESSIONAL GROWTH

Embracing the potential of artificial intelligence isn't about fearing job displacement, it's about recognizing the incredible opportunities AI unlocks for personal and professional advancement. AI is not a replacement for human ingenuity; it's a powerful tool that amplifies it. With the right approach, AI becomes not a threat, but a catalyst for growth.

Boosting Productivity Through AI

Start by considering how AI can **supercharge your productivity**. Many of the repetitive tasks that eat up your time, scheduling meetings, managing emails, drafting routine documents, can now be automated or assisted with AI. Tools like intelligent email filters, smart calendar assistants, and AI-powered writing programs help you focus on high-value tasks like problem-solving, planning, and creative thinking.

For example, instead of sifting through hundreds of emails, an AI assistant can prioritize messages, flag important conversations, and even suggest responses to common inquiries. This frees you to spend more time building relationships, solving complex challenges, or developing strategic initiatives.

Enhancing Collaboration and Teamwork

AI also transforms how we **collaborate and work in teams**. Project management platforms now use AI to track progress, flag potential bottlenecks, and suggest optimal task assignments based on team capacity. Communication tools can automatically translate across languages, summarize discussions, and detect potential misunderstandings.

In practice, marketing teams use AI to personalize campaigns by analyzing consumer behavior. Engineers employ predictive algorithms to identify maintenance needs before breakdowns occur. Designers generate multiple concepts in seconds using AI-assisted visualization tools. Across industries, AI is enhancing team performance, not replacing it.

Empowering Daily Life with Smart Tools

Outside of work, AI can improve **personal well-being** and free up valuable time. Fitness trackers deliver personalized workout suggestions. Smart home systems adjust lighting, temperature, or energy use based on your habits. Language learning apps adapt to your pace and style, making education more efficient and enjoyable.

These tools reduce stress, optimize routines, and create more space in your life for relationships, hobbies, and personal development.

Choosing the Right Tools with Intention

Harnessing AI effectively starts with a **strategic mindset**. Don't adopt every new tool indiscriminately. Instead, identify areas where automation or AI assistance would create the biggest impact. Focus on time-consuming, repetitive, or data-intensive tasks.

Evaluate AI tools based on your specific goals. Consider factors like ease of use, integration with your current tools, cost, privacy, and long-term support. Always prioritize solutions that enhance your work, rather than attempt to replace it entirely. The goal is to **work smarter, not harder**.

Understanding the Capabilities—and Limits—of AI

While AI is powerful, it's not infallible. AI systems are only as good as the data they're trained on. If that data is biased or incomplete, the system may produce flawed or unfair outcomes. That's why **human oversight and critical thinking** are essential.

Whenever possible, verify AI outputs, especially when making high-stakes decisions. Understand how the system works and question any results that seem off. A well-informed human partner remains a necessary check on machine-generated insights.

Committing to Lifelong Learning

Technology evolves rapidly. Staying ahead means committing to **lifelong learning**. Take online courses in areas like data science, AI ethics, or machine learning. Attend webinars or workshops. Explore how emerging tools apply to your industry or interests.

By continuously updating your skills and staying engaged with new developments, you remain competitive, informed, and adaptable in an AI-driven world.

Strengthening Professional Skills with AI

AI can help you sharpen your professional skill set. Writers can use AI for grammar and style refinement, or even to brainstorm content ideas. Designers can accelerate their workflow with AI image generators and layout tools. Managers can streamline team coordination and performance tracking with AI-powered dashboards.

Regardless of your role, there's likely an AI application that can **amplify your impact**. Identify where you could benefit from assistance, then explore tools tailored to those needs.

Learning with—and from—Your Community

Your AI journey doesn't have to be solitary. Join forums, professional groups, or attend industry conferences. Sharing experiences, asking questions, and collaborating with others will deepen your understanding and keep you inspired.

Connecting with others fosters **shared innovation** and helps you stay current as tools and best practices evolve.

Keeping Ethics Front and Center

As AI becomes more pervasive, **ethical considerations** must be part of your approach. Be aware of how data is collected and used. Understand issues around algorithmic bias, surveillance, and misinformation.

Use AI responsibly, advocate for fairness and transparency, and support technologies that align with your values. Ethics is not just a compliance issue, it's central to building trustworthy and sustainable systems.

Soft Skills Still Matter

No matter how advanced AI becomes, **soft skills remain essential**. Communication, emotional intelligence, empathy, and teamwork are qualities that machines cannot replicate. These human skills will define your ability to lead, collaborate, and make a lasting impact in any field.

AI may process data, but it's people who provide context,

purpose, and meaning.

Start Small and Build Strategically

You don't have to become an AI expert overnight. Begin by experimenting with one or two tools that genuinely interest you. Track the impact on your workflow, then adjust and expand your strategy as needed. The process of integrating AI is a gradual one—an **evolution, not a race**.

The key is to remain proactive, curious, and open to new ways of thinking. With this mindset, AI becomes an enabler of your goals—not an obstacle to them.

ACKNOWLEDGMENTS

First and foremost, I want to thank my wife. This book would not have been possible without your support, patience, and unwavering belief in what we're building together. Through every late night and creative detour, you've stood beside me— not only as a partner in life but also as a true collaborator in this project. Working together both professionally and personally, has taught me that resilience, love, and vision can coexist—and thrive—even in times of uncertainty.

To my child: my hope is that when you're older and navigating a world even more shaped by artificial intelligence than today, this book will serve as a guide. Not just for understanding the technology, but for recognizing the responsibility that comes with using it. I hope it helps you ask better questions, make thoughtful decisions, and stay grounded in what matters most: empathy, ethics, and human connection.

To my family, scattered across the United States and Mexico, thank you for your encouragement, curiosity, and steady belief in my work. Your support has given me the freedom to take risks and follow this path. And to my friends: thank you for the conversations that challenged me, the ideas that sparked new directions, and the laughter that kept me going.

This book was built on research, reflection, and a love of learning, but it stands on the shoulders of those who kept me anchored. I'm grateful beyond words.

—H.S.

FUTURE-READINESS CHECKLIST: A STEP-BY-STEP GUIDE TO PREPARING FOR THE AI ERA

The previous chapters emphasized the importance of ethical AI development and individual advocacy. But what does it mean, practically speaking, to be "ready" for the age of artificial intelligence? How can you proactively prepare for an increasingly AI-driven world? This chapter offers a concrete, ten-step checklist to help you not only adapt to change but thrive within it.

Step 1: Understand the Basics of AI

Before navigating the future, you need to understand the present. A foundational grasp of AI—its core concepts, how it works, and where it's applied—is essential. Fortunately, this doesn't require a computer science degree. Free and accessible resources abound, including courses on platforms like Coursera and edX, documentaries, podcasts, and introductory books.

Focus on familiarizing yourself with terms like **machine learning**, **deep learning**, **neural networks**, and **algorithms**.

Understand the difference between **narrow AI** (task-specific) and the more theoretical **general AI** (human-level intelligence). This foundational knowledge enables you to critically evaluate news stories, emerging tools, and societal implications.

Step 2: Identify Where AI Already Exists in Your Life

AI is not a distant concept—it's already embedded in your everyday routine. Whether it's your streaming service's recommendation engine, the predictive text on your phone, or the facial recognition feature that unlocks your device, AI is already shaping your experience.

Take time to inventory the tools and services you use that incorporate AI. Reflect on how they influence your choices, habits, or even opinions. Are your feeds reinforcing certain biases? Are the tools genuinely helpful or subtly intrusive? This awareness helps you become a more discerning and empowered user.

Step 3: Develop AI Literacy

AI literacy is more than just technical understanding—it's about becoming **critical and informed**. Learn to recognize misleading or manipulated AI-generated content, such as deepfakes or clickbait headlines created by generative models.

Practice verifying content through trusted sources. Understand how AI algorithms work, what data they are trained on, and how bias can be introduced. Developing this lens helps you identify misinformation and advocate for responsible media consumption.

Step 4: Embrace Lifelong Learning

The AI landscape evolves rapidly. Continuous education isn't optional—it's essential. Follow trusted AI news outlets, subscribe to thought leaders' newsletters, and enroll in short courses to build knowledge in areas like **data ethics**, **AI and society**, or **automation in the workplace**.

Lifelong learning fosters adaptability and keeps your skills sharp, whether you're looking to upskill for your current role or pivot to new opportunities.

Step 5: Strengthen Your Critical Thinking

Critical thinking is a future-proof skill. AI can automate data analysis and generate content, but only humans can **interpret**, **question**, and **contextualize**.

Don't accept information—or the AI tools themselves—at face value. Examine the sources of data. Ask whether the system serves the public good or just a commercial interest. Challenge the assumptions embedded in algorithms, and remain skeptical until claims are supported by multiple perspectives.

Step 6: Explore AI Tools to Boost Productivity and Creativity

AI tools can be powerful allies. From writing assistants and code generators to graphic design and project management platforms, explore technologies that complement your personal and professional goals.

Try tools like ChatGPT for brainstorming or copyediting, Midjourney for visual creativity, or AI-powered research platforms for accelerated learning. Learn not just how to use these tools, but how to use them responsibly and effectively.

Step 7: Engage in Ethical Conversations About AI

The ethical implications of AI are vast: bias, privacy, surveillance, labor disruption, and more. Start engaging with these topics now. Join online communities, attend webinars, or participate in local workshops focused on AI ethics.

Contributing to the conversation—whether casually or professionally—helps shape the direction of innovation. The goal isn't to be an expert, but an informed participant in the public discourse.

Step 8: Advocate for Responsible AI

You don't need a platform to make an impact. Advocacy can take many forms: contacting legislators, supporting ethical tech organizations, or simply raising awareness within your social and professional circles.

Support transparency in algorithmic decision-making, demand privacy safeguards, and push for oversight where it's lacking. Every voice adds momentum to the movement for a more equitable AI future.

Step 9: Embrace Change and Stay Adaptable

AI is transforming work, and some roles will be automated. But new opportunities are emerging just as quickly. Be ready to **pivot**, **reskill**, and **reimagine** your career path.

Whether you're in healthcare, education, marketing, or logistics, look for emerging tools and roles that align with your experience. Seek out future-facing skills like data interpretation, digital literacy, and collaboration with intelligent systems.

Step 10: Stay Informed and Engaged

The conversation around AI is just beginning. Stay plugged

into key developments—both technical and ethical. Continue building your knowledge, engaging in public dialogue, and adapting your practices.

Follow AI thought leaders, read interdisciplinary research, and join communities of practice. Being informed makes you resilient; being engaged makes you impactful.

A Living Checklist for the AI Era

This checklist isn't meant to be completed once and forgotten, it's a **living document**, a guide for continuous growth. AI will continue evolving, and so must we. By embracing lifelong learning, critical awareness, and ethical engagement, you position yourself not just to survive in the AI era, but to lead within it.

Your future-readiness isn't just personal. It's part of a collective movement toward a smarter, more inclusive, and more responsible technological future.

GLOSSARY OF KEY TERMS AND TOOLS

AI (Artificial Intelligence): A field of computer science focused on creating machines capable of performing tasks that typically require human intelligence, such as learning, problem-solving, and decision-making.

Algorithm: A set of instructions or rules followed by a computer to perform a specific task. In AI, algorithms are used to process data and generate predictions or decisions.

Autonomous Vehicle: A vehicle equipped with AI systems and sensors that enable it to navigate and operate without direct human control.

Bias (Algorithmic Bias): Systematic error in an AI system that results from prejudiced data or flawed model design, often leading to unfair or discriminatory outcomes.

ChatGPT: An AI-powered language model developed by OpenAI that can generate human-like text, answer questions, and assist with a variety of writing tasks.

Cloud Computing: The delivery of computing services—including storage, databases, and AI tools—over the internet, allowing scalable and on-demand access to technology.

Convolutional Neural Network (CNN): A type of deep learning model particularly effective in image recognition and processing.

Coursera: An online learning platform that offers courses, certificates, and degrees in a wide range of subjects, including AI and data science.

Critical Thinking: The process of analyzing and evaluating information in a disciplined and reflective manner. In the context of AI, this skill helps individuals assess algorithmic outputs and identify biases.

Data Privacy: The protection of personal data from unauthorized access, use, or disclosure, particularly important in AI systems that rely on large datasets.

Data Science: A field that uses scientific methods, processes, algorithms, and systems to extract knowledge and insights from structured and unstructured data.

Deep Learning: A subset of machine learning involving neural networks with many layers, enabling the analysis of complex patterns in data.

Deepfake: An AI-generated video or audio recording that has been manipulated to impersonate real people, often used in disinformation campaigns.

Digital Literacy: The ability to use and understand digital tools, systems, and data, including recognizing misinformation and understanding ethical concerns.

Explainable AI (XAI): A field within AI that focuses on making AI decision-making processes transparent and understandable to humans.

GitHub Copilot: An AI-powered code completion tool developed by GitHub and OpenAI that assists developers by suggesting code in real-time.

Grammarly: An AI-driven writing assistant that helps users improve grammar, clarity, tone, and style in written communication.

Lidar (Light Detection and Ranging): A sensor technology used in autonomous vehicles to measure distance and map surroundings using laser light.

Machine Learning (ML): A branch of AI that enables computers to learn patterns from data and improve over time without being explicitly programmed.

Midjourney: An AI image-generation tool that operates via Discord, allowing users to create artwork and illustrations by inputting text prompts.

Neural Network: A machine learning model inspired by the human brain, composed of interconnected nodes ("neurons") that process information.

OpenAI: A leading artificial intelligence research and deployment company dedicated to ensuring that general AI benefits all of humanity.

Path Planning: In autonomous vehicles, the process of selecting an optimal route from a starting point to a destination.

ProWritingAid: An AI-powered writing tool that offers suggestions for grammar, clarity, structure, readability, and more, commonly used by writers and editors.

Radar (Radio Detection and Ranging): A detection system that uses radio waves to determine the location, speed, and direction of objects, commonly used in autonomous vehicles.

Recurrent Neural Network (RNN): A type of neural network designed to recognize patterns in sequences of data, such as text or time-series information.

Smart City: An urban area that uses AI and connected technologies to improve infrastructure, public services, traffic management, and sustainability.

Tabnine: An AI coding assistant that helps software developers by providing real-time code completions and suggestions.

Traffic Management System: A digital infrastructure, often powered by AI, designed to monitor, predict, and regulate traffic flows in urban environments.

Transparency: In AI ethics, the principle that systems should be designed so that users can understand how decisions are made and what data is used.

Udacity: An online education platform offering nanodegree programs and courses in technical subjects including AI, programming, and data analysis.

Ultrasonic Sensor: A sensor that measures distance using sound waves, often used in vehicles for close-range detection such as parking assistance.

LEGAL DISCLAIMER

The information presented in this book is intended for general educational and informational purposes only. While every effort has been made to ensure the accuracy, completeness, and timeliness of the content, the authors and publishers make no representations or warranties of any kind, express or implied, regarding the reliability, applicability, or suitability of the information contained herein.

The field of artificial intelligence and related technologies is rapidly evolving. As such, some information, tools, or developments discussed in this book may change or become outdated over time. Readers are encouraged to consult additional sources and seek professional advice where appropriate, particularly in matters involving legal, financial, medical, or technical decisions.

Neither the author nor the publisher shall be held liable for any loss, injury, or damage allegedly arising from the use or misuse of the information contained in this publication. All product names, software, organizations, and trademarks mentioned in this book are the property of their respective owners and are used for identification purposes only. Their inclusion does not imply endorsement or affiliation.

By reading this book, you agree to use the information responsibly and understand that it is provided without warranty of any kind.